Key Stage 3 Science

Spectrum 9

Andy Cooke

Jean Martin

CAMBRIDGE
UNIVERSITY PRESS

Series editors	Andy Cooke
	Jean Martin

Consultant	Sam Ellis

Authors	David Acaster
	Trevor Bavage
	Darren Beardsley
	Chris Christofi
	Zoe Crompton
	Sam Ellis
	Kevin Frobisher
	David Glover
	Jean Martin
	Sue McCarthy
	Mick Mulligan
	Nicky Thomas
	Doug Wilford

PUBLISHED BY THE PRESS SYNDICATE OF THE UNIVERSITY OF CAMBRIDGE
The Pitt Building, Trumpington Street, Cambridge, United Kingdom

CAMBRIDGE UNIVERSITY PRESS
The Edinburgh Building, Cambridge CB2 2RU, UK
40 West 20th Street, New York, NY 10011-4211, USA
477 Williamstown Road, Port Melbourne, VIC 3207, Australia
Ruiz de Alarcón 13, 28014 Madrid, Spain
Dock House, The Waterfront, Cape Town 8001, South Africa

http://www.cambridge.org

First published 2003
Reprinted 2004

Printed in the United Kingdom by Cambridge University Press

Typeface Delima MT   *System* QuarkXPress®

A catalogue record for this book is available from the British Library

ISBN 0 521 75010 5   paperback

Cover design by Blue Pig Design Co
Page make-up and illustration by Hardlines Ltd, Charlbury, Oxford

Contents

About the *Spectrum* class book

This *Spectrum* Class Book covers what you will learn about science and scientists in Year 9. It is split into twelve **Units**. Each Unit starts with a page like this:

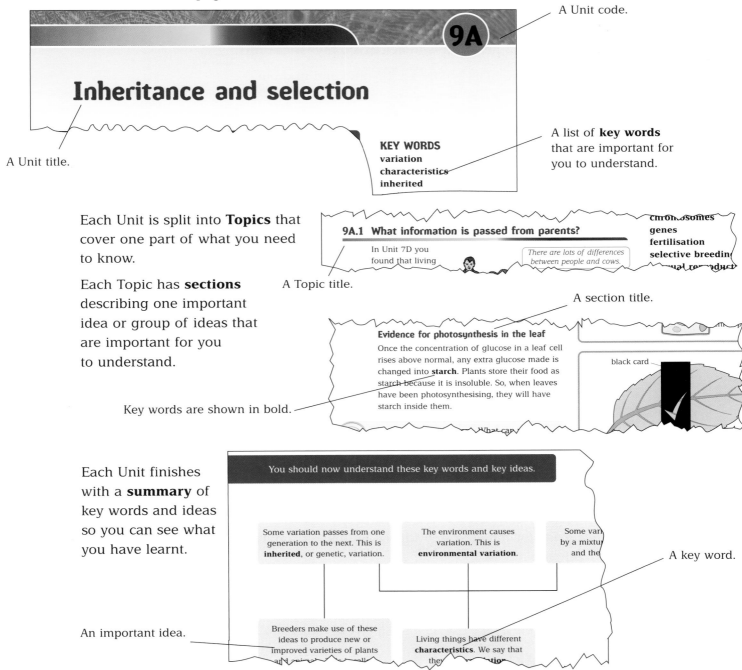

A Unit code.

9A

Inheritance and selection

KEY WORDS
variation
characteristics
inherited

A list of **key words** that are important for you to understand.

A Unit title.

Each Unit is split into **Topics** that cover one part of what you need to know.

Each Topic has **sections** describing one important idea or group of ideas that are important for you to understand.

9A.1 What information is passed from parents?

In Unit 7D you found that living

There are lots of differences between people and cows.

chromosomes
genes
fertilisation
selective breeding
...

A Topic title.

A section title.

Evidence for photosynthesis in the leaf
Once the concentration of glucose in a leaf cell rises above normal, any extra glucose made is changed into **starch**. Plants store their food as starch because it is insoluble. So, when leaves have been photosynthesising, they will have starch inside them.

black card

Key words are shown in bold.

Each Unit finishes with a **summary** of key words and ideas so you can see what you have learnt.

You should now understand these key words and key ideas.

Some variation passes from one generation to the next. This is **inherited**, or genetic, variation.

The environment causes variation. This is **environmental variation**.

Some var... by a mixtu... and the...

A key word.

An important idea.

Breeders make use of these ideas to produce new or improved varieties of plants ...

Living things have different **characteristics**. We say that they ...

v

Icons

 Telling you where to look in the Class Book to help with activities.

 Asking questions about what you have just learnt.

 Asking questions that help you think about what you have just learnt.

 Asking questions that might need some research to answer.

At the end of the book

At the end of the book you will find:

- pages 159 to 169 to help you with **scientific investigations**.

- a **glossary/index** to help you look up words and find out their meanings.

Other components of *Spectrum*

Your teacher has other components of *Spectrum* that they can use to help you learn. They have:

- a **Teacher file** or **Teacher CD-ROM** full of information for them and lots of activities of different kinds for you. The activities are split into three levels: **support**, **main** and **extension**. Some of the activities are **suitable for homework**;

- an **assessment CD-ROM** with an **analysis tool**. The CD-ROM has **multiple choice tests** to find out what you know before you start a Unit and for you to do during or after a Unit. It also has some end of year **SAT-style tests**;

- a set of **Technician Notes** with information about **practical activities**;

(and free on the web available at www.cambridge.org/spectrum)
- general guidance documents on aspects of the Science Framework;

- **investigation checklists**, **investigation sheets** – writing frames to help with structuring investigations, and **level descriptors** covering **Planning**, **Observation**, **Analysis**, **Evaluation** and **Communication**;

- **mapping grids** for the **Five Key Ideas**, **Numeracy**, **Literacy**, **ICT**, **Citizenship** and **Sc1**;

- **flash cards** for use as a revision aid or for card chases using the Year 9 key words;

- **Five Key Ideas cards** for use as a revision aid and to build giant concept maps.

Inheritance and selection

In this unit we shall be looking at how genetic information is passed on from generation to generation. We shall also look at how humans sometimes control this information to their advantage.

KEY WORDS
variation
characteristics
inherited
environmental variation
chromosomes
genes
fertilisation
selective breeding
asexual reproduction
clones

9A.1 What information is passed from parents?

In Unit 7D you found that living organisms vary. Even within the same species, animals and plants have differences. We say that they show **variation**.

There are lots of differences between people and cows.

Non-identical twins.

1 Write down <u>two</u> differences between the human and the cow.

Some differences are less obvious.

2 Write down <u>two</u> differences between the non-identical twins.

The things you described in your answers to questions 1 and 2 are called **characteristics**. These characteristics are passed from parents to offspring. We say they are **inherited**.

3 Write down <u>two</u> characteristics that the children in this family have inherited from their parents.

A family photograph

Are all characteristics inherited?

The young identical twins in the picture have inherited their characteristics from their parents.

Young identical twins

The second picture shows adult identical twins. They are quite different from each other. The environment caused these differences. So this is called **environmental variation**.

4   Write down <u>two</u> differences between the twins that are examples of environmental variation.

5   Look at the photograph of a member of four generations of one family. Write down:

  a <u>two</u> inherited characteristics;

  b <u>two</u> characteristics that you can see in the photograph that are affected by the environment.

Adult identical twins

9A.2 Why are we similar but not identical?

A complicated set of chemical instructions is needed to build your body. Your body cell nuclei contain these instructions. Each nucleus contains 23 pairs (that is, a total of 46) **chromosomes**. Small sections of these chromosomes are called **genes**. Each gene carries the instructions for a particular characteristic. So genes are coded instructions that make up your genetic material.

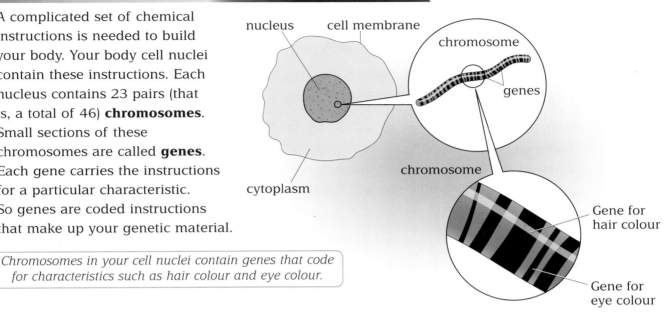

Chromosomes in your cell nuclei contain genes that code for characteristics such as hair colour and eye colour.

1   Which part of the cell contains the genetic information?

2   How many chromosomes are in a normal body cell?

In Unit 7B, you learned that the human sex cells are sperm from a man and egg cells from a woman. Sperm and egg cell nuclei each contain 23 chromosomes. The diagram shows how they are made.

How the nuclei of sex cells are made.

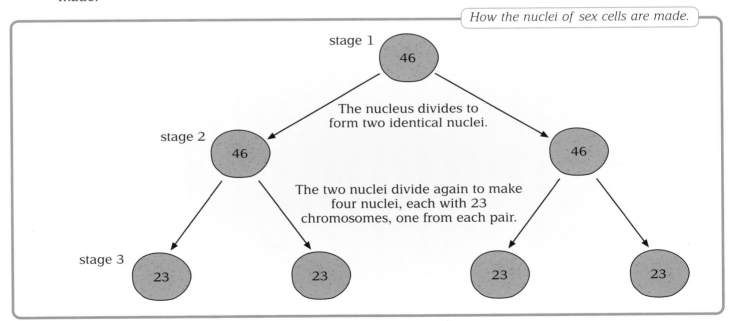

stage 1
46

The nucleus divides to form two identical nuclei.

stage 2
46   46

The two nuclei divide again to make four nuclei, each with 23 chromosomes, one from each pair.

stage 3
23   23   23   23

3   What happens to the number of chromosomes in each nucleus between stage 2 and stage 3?

Passing on the instructions

For a new life to begin, a nucleus from a sperm must join with a nucleus from an egg cell. This is called **fertilisation**.

The diagram shows the nucleus of a sperm joining with the nucleus of an egg cell. The new cell receives genetic information from both cells. This makes the new cell unique, because it contains some information from the mother and some from the father. The characteristics of the new life will be a selection from both of those parents. So sexual reproduction results in variation.

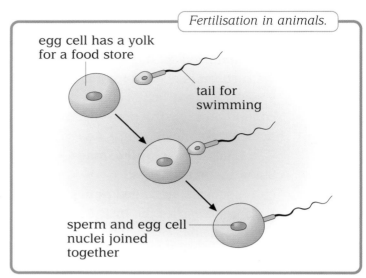

Fertilisation in animals.

egg cell has a yolk for a food store

tail for swimming

sperm and egg cell nuclei joined together

4 How are sperm cells adapted to reach egg cells?

5 How are egg cells different from many other cells in the body?

6 Why is a child not identical to either its father or its mother?

7 Use the information from the diagram to explain why a sperm cell and an egg cell each contain 23 chromosomes, but the cell after fertilisation contains 23 pairs of chromosomes.

Fertilisation in plants

Sexual reproduction in plants also involves a male and a female nucleus joining together. These nuclei also contain genetic information.
Male sex cells are inside pollen grains. Female sex cells are inside ovules.

8 How is fertilisation in plants similar to fertilisation in animals?

9 Explain why the new plant that grows from each embryo is unique.

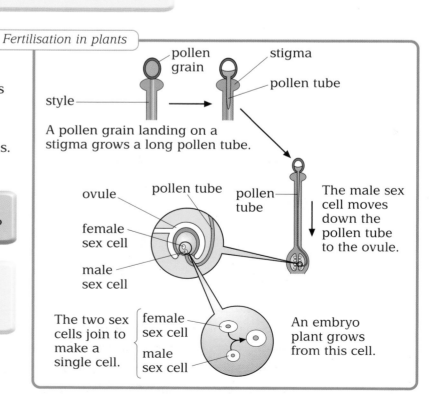

Fertilisation in plants

pollen grain

stigma

pollen tube

style

A pollen grain landing on a stigma grows a long pollen tube.

ovule

pollen tube

pollen tube

The male sex cell moves down the pollen tube to the ovule.

female sex cell

male sex cell

The two sex cells join to make a single cell.

female sex cell

male sex cell

An embryo plant grows from this cell.

9A.3 Differences between offspring

Different species of plants and animals look different.
Even members of the same species look different in many ways.
We say that they vary.

1 Look at the picture. Write down <u>two</u> ways in which the
   tomatoes are different from each other.

The yellow tomatoes come from seeds of yellow tomatoes. Tomato
colour is passed from generation to generation. It is inherited.

2 What type of seed produces red tomatoes?

3 Write down <u>one</u> characteristic not shown in the picture that
   may be passed from generation to generation in tomatoes.

4 Explain why tomato A is bigger than tomato B on
   August 4th, but they are the same size on August 12th.

Sometimes tomatoes with identical inherited characteristics are
different. The environment caused these differences.

5 Write down <u>two</u> environmental conditions
   that can affect how well a plant grows.

*Different varieties
of tomatoes.*

*On August 4th, tomato A is bigger
than tomato B. On August 12th, they
are both fully grown and are the same
size. To grow, plants need sunlight,
water, carbon dioxide and minerals.*

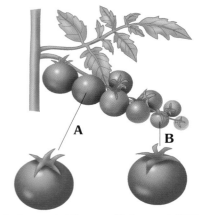

A August 4th   **B** August 12th

Patrick's experiment

> I grew some plants using seeds from one plant. I had
> some problems. There were so many plants that I had
> to keep some next to the window and some on a shelf.
> Sometimes I forgot to water them. After 6 weeks I
> measured the heights of the plants.

6 Draw a bar chart of Patrick's results.

7 The differences between Patrick's plants could have been
   caused by inheritance, by the environment or a mixture
   of both. What do you think? Explain your answer.

8 Imagine that you are Patrick's teacher. Write him a note
   explaining how to make his experiment a fair test.

Height of plant (cm)	Number of plants
31–40	6
41–50	10
51–60	15
61–70	12
71–80	8

Patrick's results

9A.4 The right breed for the right job

Even though they look different, the animals in the picture belong to the same species. Breeders have selected dogs with certain characteristics and allowed them to breed. Some examples of characteristics they have selected are size, colour and thickness of coat.

1 Look at the picture. Write down <u>two</u> ways in which the dogs are:

    a alike;

    b different.

2 **a** Which of these dogs do hunters and poachers use to bring animals out of their burrows?

    b Write down <u>two</u> characteristics of the dog that make it suitable for this job.

Selecting individuals with the most suitable characteristics and breeding from them is called **selective breeding**. There is evidence that humans domesticated a few wolves in Asia tens of thousands of years ago. Over the millennia, they developed all the different varieties of dogs from just these few wolves by selective breeding.

How selective breeding works

When animals breed naturally, they choose their own mates. Genes for lots of different characteristics are mixed over and over again. It's a bit like shuffling cards and dealing them out. You never know which characteristics will appear in each hand of cards.

In selective breeding, humans decide which animals will mate. Humans choose animals with the characteristics that they want. Think of it like choosing your cards instead of relying on chance.

3 When animals breed, a sperm cell from the male fertilises an egg cell in the female. What part of a cell contains the genes that control an animal's characteristics?

What breeders do.

Choose, from the animals that they have, male and female animals with the characteristics that they want.

↓

Breed from these animals.

↓

Select the offspring with the required characteristics and breed from them.

↓

Repeat for several generations.

Farmer Mansfield wants to breed goats with longer, softer coats.

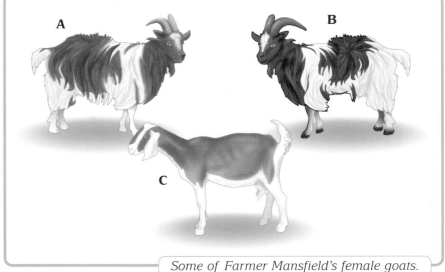

Some of Farmer Mansfield's female goats.

4 Look at the picture of the female goats. Which two goats will Farmer Mansfield let the male mate with?

5 How will the farmer decide which of the baby goats to keep and which to sell?

6 What is the next step in the breeding programme? Explain your answer.

7 Why do breeders make sure that both the male and female animals have the required characteristics before they allow them to breed?

8 Explain why breeders try to control the environmental conditions for the breeding animals.

Why humans produce new breeds

Selective breeding benefits humans in many ways. For example, Farmer Mansfield expects to be able to get more money for the hair from his goats if it is softer and longer.

9 Look at the pictures. Choose <u>two</u> examples and explain why the characteristics are useful for consumers.

10 What characteristics do you think that farmers try to develop in:

  a apples;

  b sheep?

Breeders select:

beef cattle to get the best taste, appearance and texture for their beef;

cows that produce more milk;

dogs for a variety of uses, such as guard dogs, guide dogs, sheepdogs and cute pets;

hens that lay more eggs.

9A.5 How new varieties of plant are produced

Plant breeders are producing new varieties of plants all the time. The different varieties of tomatoes shown on page 5 and the beans on this page were all produced by selective breeding.

Farmer Kirkby's bean plants varied.

1 Look at the pictures of Farmer Kirkby's plants. Write down:

a the useful characteristics of the tall plant;

b the useful characteristics of the small plant.

This plant is tall and has a strong stem but produces only a small amount of fruit. It can survive in strong winds and cold weather.

This plant is small but produces very big fruits. Strong winds and cold weather damage it.

Farmer Kirkby wanted tall, strong plants that yield lots of fruit. She produced them by selective breeding. She chose the plants that were most like the ones that she wanted and transferred pollen from one plant to the other. After several generations, she had bred offspring with the characteristics that she wanted.

Look at the diagram.

2 Farmer Kirkby did not get the type of plant that she wanted straight away. What other combinations of characteristics did her first set of plants have?

3 Which of this first set of plants did Farmer Kirkby breed from, and why?

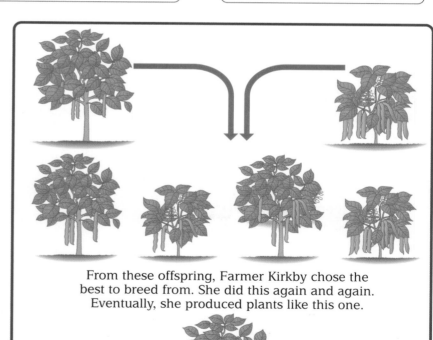

From these offspring, Farmer Kirkby chose the best to breed from. She did this again and again. Eventually, she produced plants like this one.

Fertilising the plant

On page 4, you saw how pollen on a stigma grows a long pollen tube. Then the male sex cell goes down the tube to the ovule and joins with the female sex cell.

> The two nuclei join together. We call this fertilisation.

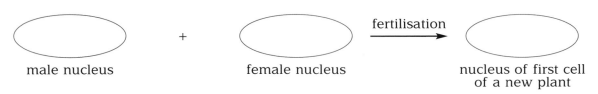

male nucleus   +   female nucleus   → fertilisation →   nucleus of first cell of a new plant

Plant breeders have to make sure that flowers are pollinated only with pollen from the plants that they have selected. It is important that plants are not pollinated by accident.

The diagram shows what plant breeders do.

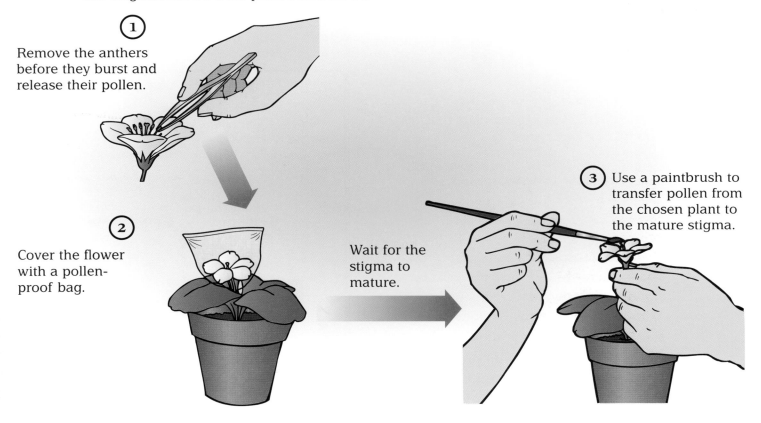

1 Remove the anthers before they burst and release their pollen.

2 Cover the flower with a pollen-proof bag.

Wait for the stigma to mature.

3 Use a paintbrush to transfer pollen from the chosen plant to the mature stigma.

4 Explain why plant breeders have to make sure that flowers are pollinated only with pollen from the plant that they have selected.

5 Explain why plant breeders use a paintbrush to transfer pollen from the chosen plant to a mature stigma.

9A.6 What is a clone?

Asexual reproduction is a type of reproduction in which only one parent is involved. The offspring have exactly the same genes as the parent. We say they are genetically identical. They are called **clones**.

1   What is a clone?

2   Write down <u>one</u> difference between asexual reproduction and sexual reproduction.

3   Describe the difference in the amount of variation resulting from sexual and asexual reproduction. Explain your answer.

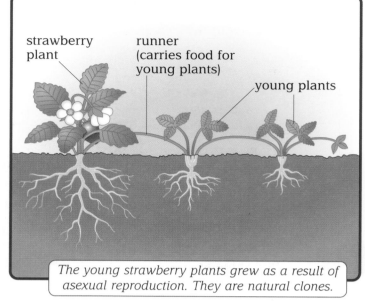

strawberry plant

runner (carries food for young plants)

young plants

The young strawberry plants grew as a result of asexual reproduction. They are natural clones.

Taking cuttings

Taking cuttings is a quick and cheap way of producing lots of new plants.

These new plants have exactly the same genes as the parent plant and as each other. So they are clones.

4   Which part of the rhubarb plant can you use to make cuttings?

5   Explain why taking cuttings is useful for a farmer who makes a living by growing rhubarb.

6   How soon would you expect the farmer to be able to harvest rhubarb from the new plants? Explain your answer.

7   A farmer grows each new rhubarb plant in the same conditions. Explain why all the plants will be identical.

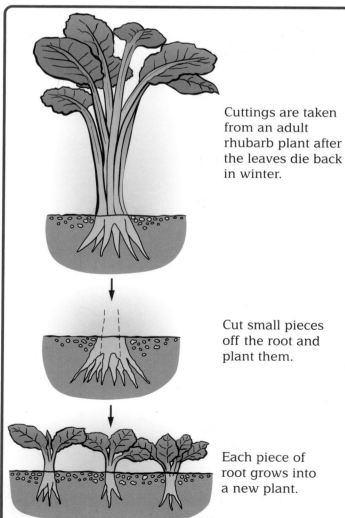

Cuttings are taken from an adult rhubarb plant after the leaves die back in winter.

Cut small pieces off the root and plant them.

Each piece of root grows into a new plant.

Producing plants by grafting

Grafting is a method of reproducing trees that gardeners use. The cut stems of two plants are taped so that the tissues grow together.

 8 Look at the diagram of plant grafting. Why are the two surfaces taped together?

Fruit trees grown from seed vary. If you plant an apple pip, it will be several years before the tree is big enough to produce apples. You will have no idea what the apples will be like. Grafted fruit trees are clones, so their characteristics are exactly the same as those of the tree from which the graft was taken.

 9 Explain the advantages of growing clones of apple trees.

Animal clones

Some tiny animals reproduce asexually and form clones. But sexual reproduction is normal in larger animals.

Scientists are finding out how to clone farm animals. Dolly the sheep was produced by cloning.

Cut a twig from the plant you want to reproduce from.

Join the twig to the stem of a rooted tree. The rooted part of the tree is called the <u>stock</u>.

— rooted stock

tape —

Tape the surfaces together. The cut heals to make a new plant.

Plant grafting

 10 Lots of people are against cloning animals such as sheep. Find out some of the reasons for this.

You should now understand these key words and key ideas.

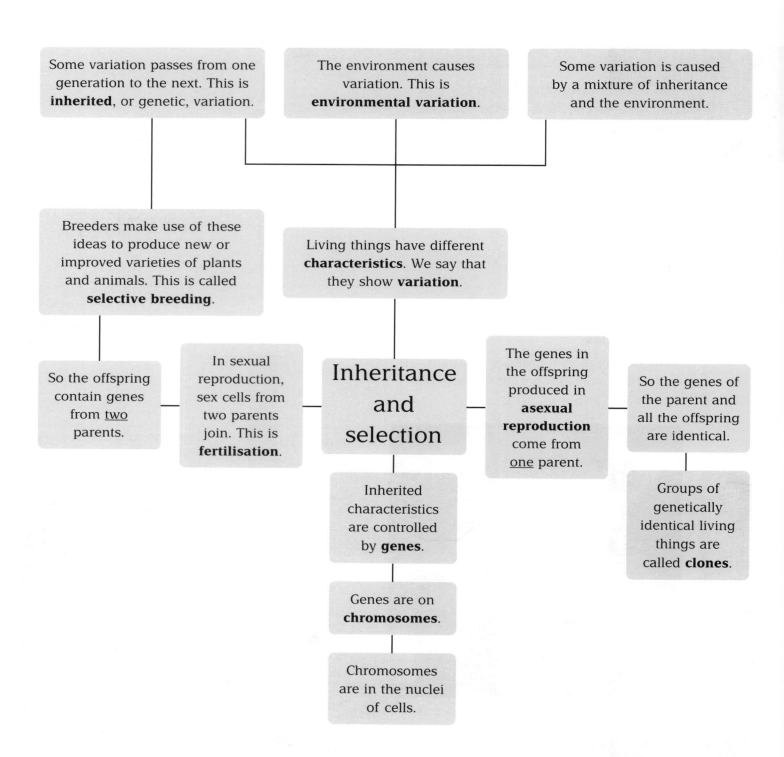

Some variation passes from one generation to the next. This is **inherited**, or genetic, variation.

The environment causes variation. This is **environmental variation**.

Some variation is caused by a mixture of inheritance and the environment.

Breeders make use of these ideas to produce new or improved varieties of plants and animals. This is called **selective breeding**.

Living things have different **characteristics**. We say that they show **variation**.

So the offspring contain genes from two parents.

In sexual reproduction, sex cells from two parents join. This is **fertilisation**.

Inheritance and selection

The genes in the offspring produced in **asexual reproduction** come from one parent.

So the genes of the parent and all the offspring are identical.

Inherited characteristics are controlled by **genes**.

Groups of genetically identical living things are called **clones**.

Genes are on **chromosomes**.

Chromosomes are in the nuclei of cells.

Fitness and health

In this unit we shall be exploring what it means to be fit and healthy, and how different parts of your body work together to keep you fit. We shall also investigate the important things that <u>you</u> can do to improve your health.

9B.1 Ideas about fitness

We often hear statements such as 'She's super-fit!', 'I really need to get fit', 'I've never been fitter!'. But we need to think about what it means to be fit.

1 Look at the photographs. Discuss the following questions in a small group before you write down your answers. Give reasons for your answers.

   a For each person, decide whether or not you think they are fit.

   b Which person shown is probably the most unfit?

A

B

C

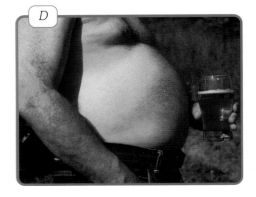
D

E

F

Fitness means different things to different people. Just because they're disabled or old doesn't mean that a person is unfit. The fat young man in the photograph is probably very unfit for his age. If you are fit, your body uses energy in an efficient way during exercise. Usually, the fitter you are, the more exercise you can do without getting tired.

2 In a small group, try to agree on a list of different kinds of fitness. Write it down.

Energy gets you going

The cells in your body require supplies of glucose and oxygen to release the energy they need.

Your skeleton and muscles work together to move your body.

Your cells use oxygen to release the energy stored in the glucose molecules. This is **respiration** and it takes place in every cell in your body.

Your <u>circulatory system</u>, including your heart and blood vessels, transports digested food and oxygen to your cells, including your muscle cells.

Your **breathing** system moves oxygen into your blood, and removes carbon dioxide from your blood.

Your <u>digestive system</u> breaks food down into simple molecules, such as glucose. These can then enter the bloodstream.

Different systems in your body work together to keep you fit.

3 Why do all your cells need glucose and oxygen? Explain this as fully as you can.

4 Look at the diagram. Write down <u>three</u> systems in your body that help to get glucose and oxygen to your cells.

5 Choose <u>one</u> of the three systems and explain briefly how your fitness is affected when that system is not working properly.

6 Write a word equation for respiration. Use the information in the diagram to help you.

Respiration takes place in every cell in your body.

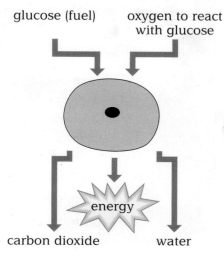

glucose (fuel)   oxygen to react with glucose

energy

carbon dioxide   water

9B.2 Breathing in action

You have learned that every cell in your body takes in oxygen for respiration and releases carbon dioxide. The air containing these gases goes into and out of your lungs when you breathe.
Your chest works a bit like a pair of bellows, drawing the air in and then forcing it out.

Place one hand on the middle of your upper chest. Place your other hand on your side, just above your waist. Take a few deep breaths.

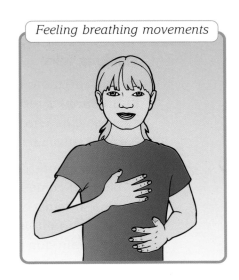

1 Describe the movements that you feel, first as you inhale (breathe in), and then as you exhale (breathe out).

Breathing in

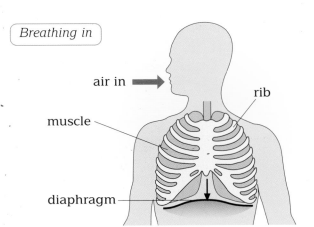

air in ➡

rib

muscle

diaphragm

Breathing out

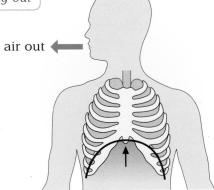

air out ⬅

- The diaphragm is a sheet of muscle that separates the chest cavity from the abdomen. When it contracts, it moves down and becomes flat. This increases the space inside the chest cavity.

- The muscles between the ribs contract, causing the ribcage to move out and up. This increases the volume of the chest cavity.

- The increase in chest volume causes air to be drawn into the lungs.

- The diaphragm relaxes. It moves up and becomes dome-shaped, decreasing the volume of the chest cavity.

- The muscles between the ribs relax, and the ribs move down and in. This decreases the size of the chest cavity.

- Air is forced out of the lungs.

2 Name four parts of your body that are involved in breathing.

3 Explain what makes air go into your lungs.

4 Which requires more effort, breathing in or breathing out? Explain why.

5 What happens to your breathing rate when you:

   a exercise;

   b go to sleep?

9B.3 The dangers of smoking

Smoking kills!

Every year, more than 100 000 people die in Britain as a result of smoking. This is because cigarette smoke contains many harmful substances.

- Carbon monoxide is the same poisonous gas that comes out of a car's exhaust pipe. It replaces oxygen in your blood so important organs such as your heart and brain don't get enough oxygen.

- Nicotine is an addictive drug that makes your body want more of it. When people's bodies become dependent on a drug, we say that they are **addicted**. Nicotine is as addictive as cocaine. It also raises the blood pressure and the heart rate, and makes the heart work harder. So the carbon monoxide and nicotine together make smokers more likely to have heart attacks and strokes. A stroke is when a clot of blood causes brain damage or death.

- Tar is a mixture of chemicals that cause **cancer** of the mouth, throat and lungs, as well as other lung conditions.

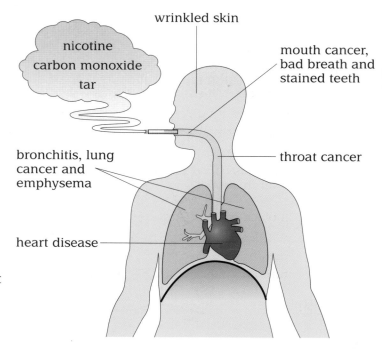

The effects of smoking are not 'cool' or exciting.

nicotine
carbon monoxide
tar

wrinkled skin

mouth cancer, bad breath and stained teeth

throat cancer

bronchitis, lung cancer and emphysema

heart disease

1 Draw a table to show the dangerous substances in cigarette smoke. In one column name the substances, and in the other column list the parts of the body that are most affected by them.

2 What does the graph show?

3 How many people (per 10 000) who don't smoke die of lung cancer?

4 How many people (per 10 000) who smoke 20 cigarettes a day die of lung cancer?

Remember, this doesn't mean that if you smoke you will get lung cancer, or that if you don't smoke you can't get lung cancer. It means that your risk of getting lung cancer increases as the number of cigarettes you smoke increases.

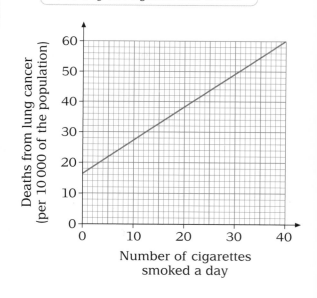

The number of deaths related to smoking in England and Wales.

Deaths from lung cancer (per 10 000 of the population)

Number of cigarettes smoked a day

How smoking damages the lungs

In the photograph you can see some lung damage caused by smoking.

In a healthy person, the cilia and mucus in the air pipes work together to keep harmful particles out of the lungs. But the poisonous substances in cigarette smoke destroy the cilia. Instead of getting swept out of the lungs, the mucus and particles trickle down into them. Smokers cough to try and get rid of the mucus, but often bacteria remain and cause an infection called **bronchitis**.

Constant coughing can break the walls of the air sacs. This reduces the surface area of the lungs, so the person struggles to get enough oxygen. We say that he or she is short of breath. This illness is called **emphysema**.

70 per cent of the tar in cigarette smoke stays in the lungs. It forms a black coating inside the tiny tubes and air sacs. Tar can make the normal cells lining the air tubes change into cancer cells. These cells divide more than normal cells, and they form a lump called a tumour. Lung cancer is difficult to cure.

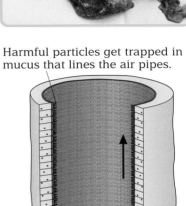

A lung of a non-smoker

A lung of a smoker

Harmful particles get trapped in mucus that lines the air pipes.

Tiny hairs called cilia move the mucus upwards and into the throat. Then you swallow it!

The lining of the air pipes is designed to keep harmful substances in the air, such as dust, bacteria and viruses, away from the lungs.

5 How does the breathing system work to stop harmful substances in air getting into the lungs?

6 Explain why smokers often cough when they wake up in the morning.

7 Find out more about either bronchitis or emphysema. In your research, include the symptoms of the illness and how it is treated.

8 Discuss the following questions and then write down your views.

   a Should smoking be banned completely?

   b Should the National Health Service (NHS) pay for a heart operation needed by a smoker?

- Cigarette smoke contains more than 4000 chemicals.
- The longer you smoke, the greater your risk of developing different cancers.
- Women who smoke during pregnancy increase their chance of miscarriage and of having very small babies.
- Smoking can cause eye and ear problems, tooth decay and weakening of bones, called osteoporosis.
- Smoking costs the NHS about £1.7 billion a year.

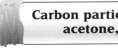

Carbon particles, arsenic, ammonia, acetone, hydrogen cyanide

The good news

The damage caused by smoking need not be permanent. If a heavy smoker stops smoking, his or her risk of getting lung cancer slowly falls. Within 10 years, that chance is the same as for a person who doesn't smoke. So, it's never too late to STOP!

9 Write down in one sentence what you believe is the most important reason never to start smoking.

9B.4 Why your diet is important

A balancing act

To be fit and healthy, it is important to eat a balanced diet. This is one that contains the right amounts of proteins, carbohydrates, fats, **vitamins** and **minerals**, fibre and water.

For centuries, scientists have been gathering evidence about how what we eat affects our health. For example, in the early 1900s a famous English scientist, Sir Frederick Gowland Hopkins, fed rats on a diet of pure carbohydrates, fats, proteins and minerals. He thought that these were all the things needed for good health. Within weeks, all the rats were dead. Another group of rats that had the same diet, but with a little milk added, all survived. Something in milk, needed in tiny amounts, kept the rats healthy. We now call these things vitamins.

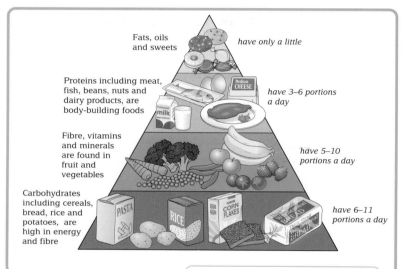

Fats, oils and sweets *have only a little*

Proteins including meat, fish, beans, nuts and dairy products, are body-building foods *have 3–6 portions a day*

Fibre, vitamins and minerals are found in fruit and vegetables *have 5–10 portions a day*

Carbohydrates including cereals, bread, rice and potatoes, are high in energy and fibre *have 6–11 portions a day*

A pyramid is an easy way of showing how much food to eat from the different groups.

1 Draw a table to summarise the main food groups and examples of foods that contain them.

2 Explain why it is better to get most of your energy from carbohydrates such as cereals, potatoes and pasta, rather than from fats, oils and sweets.

3 Plan a healthy, balanced picnic meal. It should taste good too! Use the pyramid to help you.

4 Explain how the evidence gathered by Sir Frederick Gowland Hopkins affects your life.

Feast or famine

Malnutrition means 'bad eating'. A malnourished person eats too much or too little of a particular food. In Britain, most malnourished people either eat the wrong foods or they eat too much food. If you take in more food energy than your body uses, the extra is stored as fat. You can become overweight or obese. To reduce your weight, you can either eat less or exercise more. You use up more energy when you exercise.

In some countries, many people die of starvation. Others suffer from kwashiorkor, which is malnutrition caused by a lack of protein. Many people worldwide have other diseases caused by a shortage of just one thing in their diet. We call these deficiency diseases.

A deficient diet can lead to many diseases or problems.

Nutrient	Sources	Symptoms of deficiency
Iron	Red meat Eggs Cereals	Anaemia: people look pale and feel weak because the blood does not carry enough oxygen
Calcium	Dairy products Dark green vegetables Sardines (bones)	Poor growth of bones and rotting teeth
Vitamin C	Citrus fruit Fresh vegetables	Scurvy: gums crack and wounds don't heal; bleeding under the skin
Vitamin D	Eggs Dairy products Fish oil Made by your skin in sunlight	Rickets: softening and bending of the bones
Protein	Meat Fish Eggs Dairy products Pulses (peas, beans, lentils)	Kwashiorkor: poor growth, swelling due to water collecting in tissues

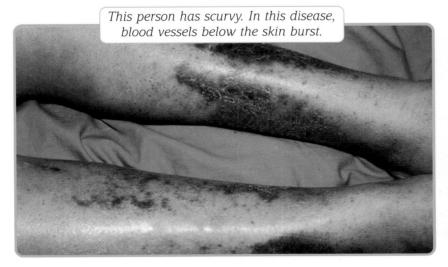

This person has scurvy. In this disease, blood vessels below the skin burst.

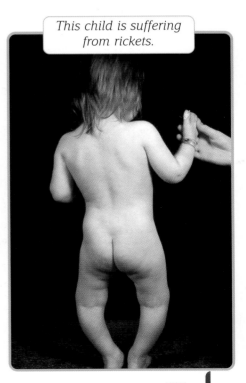

This child is suffering from rickets.

5   Explain what you need to add to your diet if:

   a your teeth often need filling and your bones break easily;

   b you are suffering from kwashiorkor.

9B.5 The use and abuse of drugs

A **drug** is any substance that changes the way your body or mind works. So alcohol, aspirin, cocaine, Ecstasy, antibiotics, nicotine, paracetamol and caffeine are all drugs. Changes to the body or mind can be helpful or harmful. Some drugs improve your mood, feelings or behaviour; others make them worse. Some drugs heal, and others damage organs in your body. Even drugs that heal can have bad effects, such as headaches and nausea. We call these side effects.

There are many different ways of grouping drugs. The diagram shows one way.

Classification of some common drugs.

DRUGS any substances that change the way the body or mind works

Legal drugs not against the law to take or sell

Illegal drugs against the law to take (unless prescribed) or sell; grouped by the way they affect the body or mind

over-the-counter drugs can be bought in shops
- painkillers
- cough mixtures
- slimming pills
- solvents

prescription drugs prescribed or ordered by a doctor
- tranquillisers
- sleeping pills
- antibiotics
- strong painkillers

recreational drugs used for enjoyment; usually socially accepted but can be very harmful
- caffeine
- nicotine
- alcohol

stimulants speed up the way the brain works; wake you up
- cocaine
- crack
- Ecstasy
- amphetamines

depressants slow down the way the brain works; put you to sleep
- opium
- morphine
- heroin
- cannabis

hallucinogens cause visions or 'hallucinations'
- cannabis
- LSD ('acid')

1   Name <u>three</u> groups of legal drugs.

2   Are any legal drugs harmful or dangerous?
    Use examples to explain your answer.

3   Write down <u>one</u> example of a drug that falls into more than one group. Explain your answer.

4   Many drugs have side effects.
    Use an example to explain what this means.

The danger of drugs

All drugs can be dangerous if they are not used in the correct way. When you use a legal drug, you should follow the instructions very carefully. If you don't, or if you use a drug prescribed for someone else, then you are misusing or abusing the drug. Abuse of legal and illegal drugs is extremely dangerous. Some reasons why are shown in the photographs.

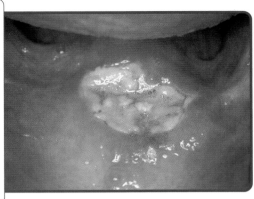

Drugs can damage cells, often in the brain, heart, liver or kidneys. Overdose of drugs causes thousands of deaths every year. This person has mouth cancer from smoking tobacco and cannabis.

Drugs such as alcohol slow reactions, causing accidents on the road, at work or in the home. One of the drivers had been drinking alcohol.

*Many drugs are addictive. This means that if you take the drug for some time, you become dependent on the drug and need it to function. If addicts stop taking drugs, they feel ill, anxious and may shake or vomit. These are called **withdrawal symptoms**.*

 5 What do we call drugs that can be taken only with a doctor's permission?

 6 Name <u>two</u> legal drugs that are addictive.

 7 Besides the three dangers of drugs mentioned, in what other harmful ways can drugs affect a person's life?

The effect of alcohol on your body

Alcohol is a drug because it changes the way your body works. It is also a poison. When you drink alcohol, it is absorbed into your bloodstream within a few minutes. It is carried to all parts of your body and begins to affect every cell.

A function of your liver is to protect your body from the harmful effects of alcohol. As the blood passes through the liver, it breaks down the alcohol into less harmful substances. It takes about one hour for a healthy liver to get rid of one unit of alcohol from the body. If the liver receives alcohol at a faster rate than this, its own cells become damaged. Drinking heavily over a long period of time can scar the liver. This is called cirrhosis and can cause death.

Children shouldn't drink alcohol. If adults choose to drink, then they should do so sensibly. Health advisers suggest an upper limit for adults of 14 units a week for women and 21 units a week for men.

Alcohol slows down the way the brain works and affects your behaviour. It can reduce your will power and control, which often leads to violence, accidents and unwanted pregnancies. It can make you sleepy and clumsy and can slur your speech. Sometimes alcohol causes loss of memory and even permanent brain damage. It also increases your blood pressure and pulse rate. Over a long period, alcohol damages the heart and increases your risk of a heart attack.

Alcohol can irritate the lining of the stomach and eventually cause stomach ulcers. Alcohol also increases the flow of blood to the skin. This makes the drinker look flushed and feel warm. In fact, the body will lose heat quickly in this situation.

When a pregnant woman drinks, alcohol passes to the baby through the placenta. Drinking too much can slow down the baby's development and even cause brain damage.

One way of comparing the amount of alcohol in different drinks is by using 'units' of alcohol as a measurement. A unit is 10ml of pure alcohol. As a rough guide:

1 unit = half a pint of beer

= one tot (25ml) of spirit, such as whisky, brandy, gin or vodka

= a small glass (125ml) of wine

= 150ml of 'alco pop'

How much is too much?

 8 List <u>four</u> organs in the body that can be damaged by alcohol.

9 Read again through the section on the effects of alcohol on the body. Summarise the main points by annotating a diagram of the human body. The first annotation has been done for you.

Some parts of the body affected by alcohol

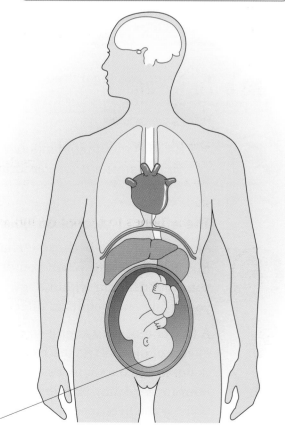

Alcohol can cause brain damage and stunt the growth of a developing fetus.

Some frightening facts

Alcohol is legal, socially acceptable and used regularly by most people in Britain. But before you decide to drink, remember the following.

- Twice as many people are addicted to alcohol as to all other drugs put together.

- Violent crime and violence in the home are often linked to alcohol.

- More than 1000 young people are admitted to hospital each year with alcohol poisoning.

- About half of adult pedestrians killed in road accidents have been drinking too much. One result is shown in the poster.

- If you drink heavily in the evening, you can still be over the legal drink-drive limit the next morning.

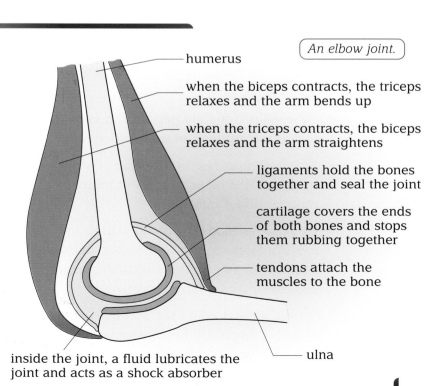

Think before you drink!

Look her in the eye. Then say a quick drink never hurt anybody.

DRINKING AND DRIVING WRECKS LIVES.

10 Use examples to explain the difference between the 'use' and 'abuse' of alcohol and other drugs.

11 Discuss and write down your views on the question 'Should alcohol be banned or more controlled, given the number of people harmed by the abuse of alcohol?'.

9B.6 Fit for life

Joints in action

The place where two bones connect is called a joint. Muscles are fixed to your bones on both sides of a joint. The muscles pull on the bones to make you move.

1 What is a joint?

2 Write a paragraph to explain how a joint works. Use the diagram to help you.

An elbow joint.

humerus

when the biceps contracts, the triceps relaxes and the arm bends up

when the triceps contracts, the biceps relaxes and the arm straightens

ligaments hold the bones together and seal the joint

cartilage covers the ends of both bones and stops them rubbing together

tendons attach the muscles to the bone

inside the joint, a fluid lubricates the joint and acts as a shock absorber

ulna

You have learned how important exercise is for keeping you fit and healthy. However, too much exercise, or the wrong kind of exercise or movement, can damage the joints and muscles.

If you twist your foot inwards suddenly, you can overstretch or tear the ligaments. A <u>sprain</u> like this causes your ankle to swell.

If you do sudden vigorous exercise, you might injure a muscle. This is called a <u>strain</u> or 'pulled muscle'. Overdoing exercise can also cause muscles to contract so powerfully that they hurt. This is called <u>cramp</u>. A 'stitch' is a type of cramp in the abdominal muscles, caused by very hard exercise.

You can reduce the chance of getting a sports injury by warming up before exercise.

 3 Explain the difference between a sprain and a strain.

 4 List some of the common causes of sports injuries.

 5 Find out about <u>one</u> of the following conditions: tennis elbow, water on the knee, dislocated hip, arthritis, slipped disc or any sports injury.

Eating and exercising for your heart

In this unit, you have looked at the effects of diet, drugs and exercise on health and fitness.

Being fit and healthy is about making the right choices. If you choose to exercise regularly, you can improve your fitness in different ways.

- Your heart is mainly muscle and exercise makes it stronger and more efficient.

- Exercise improves the strength of your muscles. This helps to prevent injury to muscles and joints.

- Exercise develops the blood vessels in muscle. More oxygen and carbon dioxide can flow to and from the muscles, so your muscles work better.

If you eat a diet high in fat, you increase your risk of **coronary heart disease**.

Coronary heart disease begins when the blood vessels in the heart become narrow because of a build-up of fatty material. This fatty material is made from cholesterol, which the body makes from fat in food.

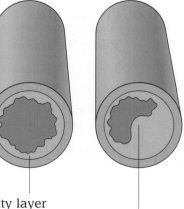

artery wall

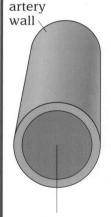

blood within normal artery

fatty layer starting to form

fatty layer, which stops the blood flowing freely. The heart muscle becomes short of oxygen, and this causes angina, which is very painful. A heart attack happens when the narrowed arteries become blocked by a blood clot.

To lower your chance of heart disease, you need to:

- eat at least five portions of fruit and vegetables a day;
- eat less fat;
- keep your weight normal, so your heart doesn't need to overwork;
- not eat too much salt, because salt raises your blood pressure.

 6 Explain the cause of angina.

 7 You are a doctor, and you are with a patient who has heart problems. List <u>five</u> questions you would ask your patient, to find out if they need to make some lifestyle changes.

Are we healthier than our great-grandparents were?

Science is about finding answers to questions. The question in the heading is a broad and general question. Scientists first break down a general question into a few smaller questions that are easier to investigate. They then plan a suitable investigation and collect the evidence. Evidence is information that can be used to make a decision or to answer a question. Lastly, they use the answers to the smaller questions to help them answer the general question.

In this unit, we have looked at many questions related to fitness and health. One final one is 'Are we healthier than our great-grandparents were?' Your first response might be 'Yes, of course we are.' But we need to investigate this general question in a scientific way – finding evidence to back up our answer. First, we need to think about differences between our lifestyles and those of our great-grandparents that might have an effect on health – different diets, for example.

Scientists develop new vaccine.

People spend more time in cars than ever before.

 8 Write down at least <u>three</u> things affecting health that were different in your great-grandparents' time. The photographs and newspaper articles will help you.

9 Write down <u>one</u> question you could investigate in a scientific way that would help you to decide whether or not we are healthier than our great-grandparents were.

You should now know these key words and ideas.

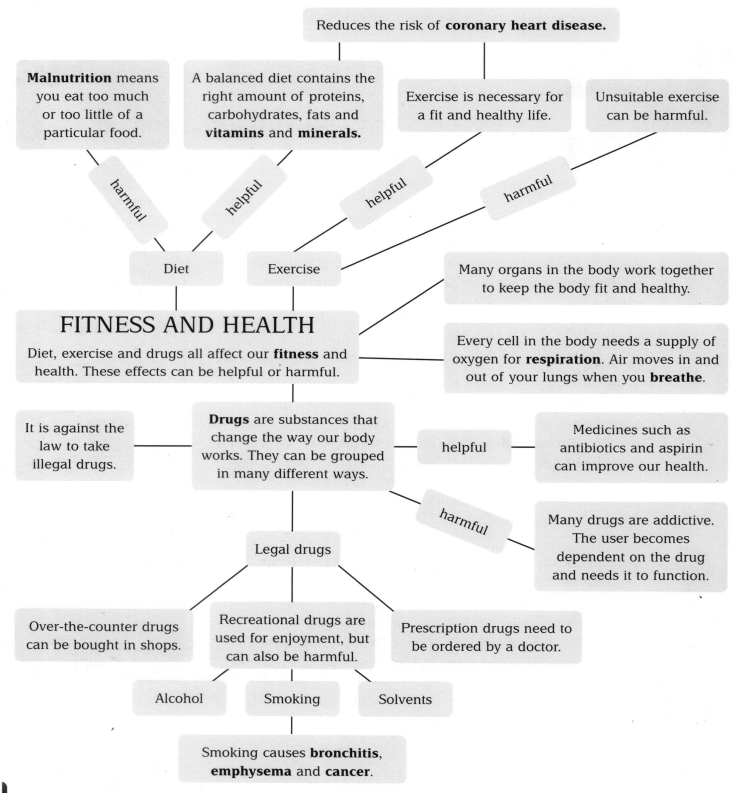

Reduces the risk of **coronary heart disease.**

Malnutrition means you eat too much or too little of a particular food.

A balanced diet contains the right amount of proteins, carbohydrates, fats and **vitamins** and **minerals.**

Exercise is necessary for a fit and healthy life.

Unsuitable exercise can be harmful.

harmful

helpful

helpful

harmful

Diet

Exercise

Many organs in the body work together to keep the body fit and healthy.

FITNESS AND HEALTH

Diet, exercise and drugs all affect our **fitness** and health. These effects can be helpful or harmful.

Every cell in the body needs a supply of oxygen for **respiration**. Air moves in and out of your lungs when you **breathe**.

It is against the law to take illegal drugs.

Drugs are substances that change the way our body works. They can be grouped in many different ways.

helpful

Medicines such as antibiotics and aspirin can improve our health.

harmful

Many drugs are addictive. The user becomes dependent on the drug and needs it to function.

Legal drugs

Over-the-counter drugs can be bought in shops.

Recreational drugs are used for enjoyment, but can also be harmful.

Prescription drugs need to be ordered by a doctor.

Alcohol

Smoking

Solvents

Smoking causes **bronchitis**, **emphysema** and **cancer**.

Plants and photosynthesis

In this unit we shall be learning about how the leaves of green plants are adapted to make food from carbon dioxide and water using light energy. We shall consider the importance of this food to humans and other animals.

KEY WORDS
photosynthesis
glucose
biomass
chloroplasts
starch
chlorophyll
root hairs
respiration
minerals
nitrates
energy
conservation

9C.1 How do plants grow?

Only green plants make food. We and other animals eat the food that plants make, or eat other animals that have fed on plants.

The leaves of plants are like little food factories.
The raw materials that they use to make food are:

● carbon dioxide, taken from the air through pores in the leaves;

● water, absorbed from the soil by the roots.

The energy for the process of making food is light. The word 'photo' means light, and the word 'synthesis' means making, so we call the process **photosynthesis**.

1 Use the information in the diagram to write a word equation.

The first substance that plants make is **glucose** (a type of sugar). Then they change the glucose into other substances. These are the materials that plants are made of. We call the mass of all these materials the **biomass** of the plant.

2 The word 'biomass' is made up of the words 'bio' and 'mass'. Use a dictionary to find out what these two words mean.

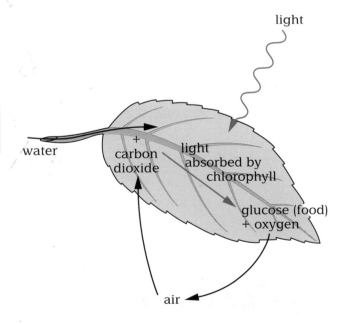

light

water

carbon dioxide

light absorbed by chlorophyll

glucose (food) + oxygen

air

What happens in a leaf

A bit of history

In the 17th century, a Dutch scientist called Jan Baptista van Helmont believed that the biomass of a plant came from just water. He planted a willow tree weighing only 1 kg in a big pot containing 90 kg of dry soil. He covered the soil with a piece of tin with lots of holes in it so that only rainwater went through it. Five years later, the tree weighed 100 kg.

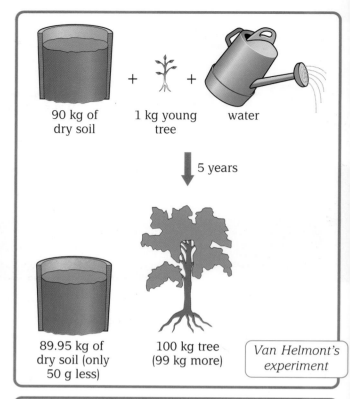

3 Van Helmont realised that plants need water to make food and to grow. Write down <u>two</u> other things that a plant needs to make its food.

4 **a** Suggest why van Helmont thought that water is enough for plants to grow.

    b What is the evidence that a plant's food does not come from the soil?

5 Eleanor told her science teacher, Mr Holmes, that she wasn't convinced by van Helmont's experiment. She still believed that plants take their food from the soil. Write a few sentences to explain to Eleanor how Mr Holmes' experiment provides evidence that a plant's food does not come from the soil.

90 kg of dry soil + 1 kg young tree + water

5 years

89.95 kg of dry soil (only 50 g less)   *100 kg tree (99 kg more)*

Van Helmont's experiment

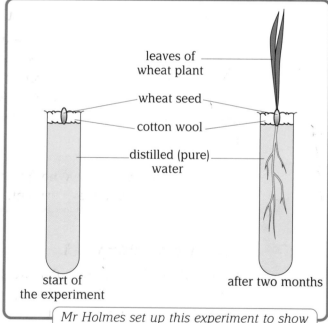

leaves of wheat plant

wheat seed

cotton wool

distilled (pure) water

start of the experiment   *after two months*

Mr Holmes set up this experiment to show Eleanor that van Helmont was right.

Daily ups and downs

6 Look at the table.

    a Describe the changes in the amount of carbon dioxide over 24 hours.

    b Suggest an explanation for these changes.

Time	2 am	5 am	8 am	11 am	2 pm	5 pm	8 pm	11 pm
CO_2 concentration (parts per million) amongst leaves	425	352	300	285	280	287	335	380

9C.2 Leaves and photosynthesis

Taking a closer look at a leaf

In a plant, the leaf is the special organ in which most photosynthesis takes place.

The diagram shows the cells in which most photosynthesis happens. These are called palisade cells.

1   Describe the shape of the palisade cells.

2   Suggest how the shape of the palisade cells helps the leaf in photosynthesis.

3   Why are most chloroplasts found near the top of the palisade cells?

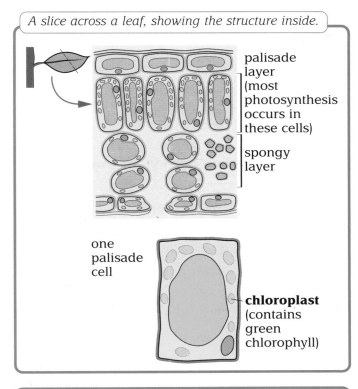

A slice across a leaf, showing the structure inside.

palisade layer (most photosynthesis occurs in these cells)

spongy layer

one palisade cell

chloroplast (contains green chlorophyll)

Evidence for photosynthesis in the leaf

Once the concentration of glucose in a leaf cell rises above normal, any extra glucose made is changed into **starch**. Plants store their food as starch because it is insoluble. So, when leaves have been photosynthesising, they will have starch inside them.

4   Look at the diagram. What can you conclude from this experiment?

The need for chlorophyll

Chlorophyll is the green substance in leaves that absorbs light. Without chlorophyll, a leaf cannot trap and use the light it needs to make food. Plants that are kept in the dark cannot make food. They end up weak and spindly.

Starch turns blue/black when iodine solution is added to it.

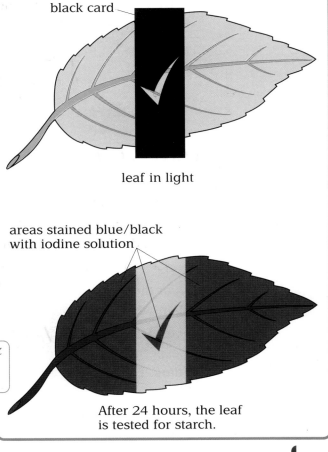

black card

leaf in light

areas stained blue/black with iodine solution

After 24 hours, the leaf is tested for starch.

Some leaves have green parts (containing chlorophyll) and white parts (not containing chlorophyll). We call them variegated leaves. Look at the diagram to see what happens when we test one of these leaves for starch.

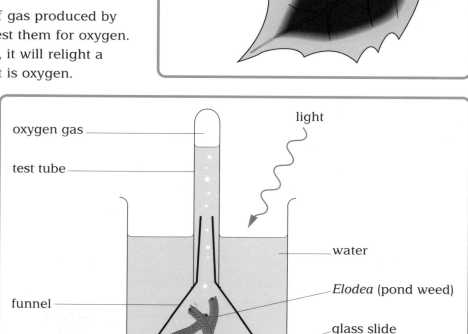

leaf before the test

leaf after testing with iodine solution

5 What evidence is there from the experiment that chlorophyll is needed to make starch?

Carbon dioxide in, oxygen out

In 1772, a man called Joseph Priestley discovered that plants produce a gas that animals need. We now know that this gas is oxygen.

We can collect the bubbles of gas produced by the water plant *Elodea* and test them for oxygen. If we can collect enough gas, it will relight a glowing splint, so we know it is oxygen.

When we do experiments, we normally set up controls. For example, when we look at the effect of water on plants, we need a control experiment where some plants are not given any water.

6 What control can we use for the experiment with *Elodea*?

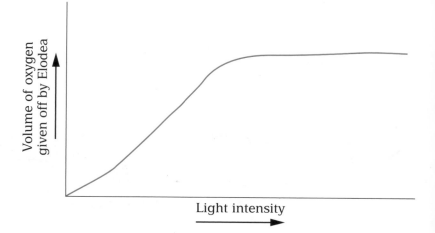

oxygen gas

light

test tube

water

Elodea (pond weed)

funnel

glass slide

How does light intensity affect the amount of oxygen produced?

7 Look at the graph. Explain what it shows.

8 Suggest what would happen if this experiment was done in the dark. Explain your answer.

Volume of oxygen given off by Elodea

Light intensity

9C.3 What happens to the glucose made in leaves?

Plants use glucose for many things.

- Making starch: plants join together lots of small glucose molecules to make long starch molecules. Starch is stored in roots, stems, leaves, fruits and seeds.

- Releasing energy in respiration: plants need this energy for their life processes.

- Making new materials such as proteins, oils and cellulose.

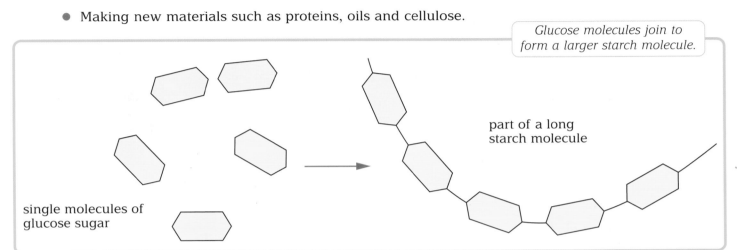

Glucose molecules join to form a larger starch molecule.

single molecules of glucose sugar

part of a long starch molecule

So, some of the glucose is used to release energy, while the rest increases the biomass of the plant.

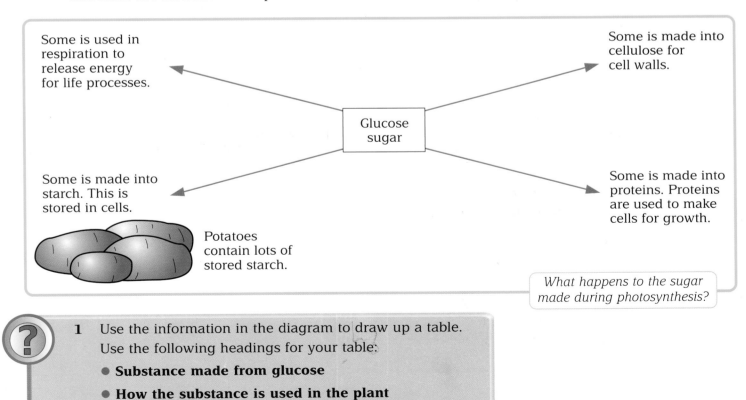

Some is used in respiration to release energy for life processes.

Some is made into cellulose for cell walls.

Glucose sugar

Some is made into starch. This is stored in cells.

Potatoes contain lots of stored starch.

Some is made into proteins. Proteins are used to make cells for growth.

What happens to the sugar made during photosynthesis?

?

1 Use the information in the diagram to draw up a table. Use the following headings for your table:
- **Substance made from glucose**
- **How the substance is used in the plant**

9C.4 Roots, water and minerals

Plant roots are important for anchorage and because they take up water from the soil. You learnt about root hairs in Unit 7A.

1   Describe the route that water takes in a plant from the soil to the leaves.

2   What do the leaves use the water for?

3   Look at the diagram. Write down <u>two</u> things that give roots a larger surface area for absorbing water.

4   How does the shape of the root hair cells help the plant take up water?

Root hair cells, like other living cells, need oxygen for **respiration**. The oxygen is needed to release energy from food for the cell's life processes.

5   Where do root cells get their oxygen for respiration?

Many plants cannot survive in flooded or waterlogged soil. Water does not have as much oxygen dissolved in it as there is oxygen in air.

Antonis is a farmer in a small village called Livadia on the south coast of Cyprus. Livadia is in a valley between the coast and the hills. For many years, when Antonis was a young man, his crops were ruined when the valley flooded. Nowadays, man-made rivers take any flood water away from the valley and into the sea.

6   Why did the flooding kill Antonis' crops?

7   Write down <u>two</u> things that roots take from the soil.

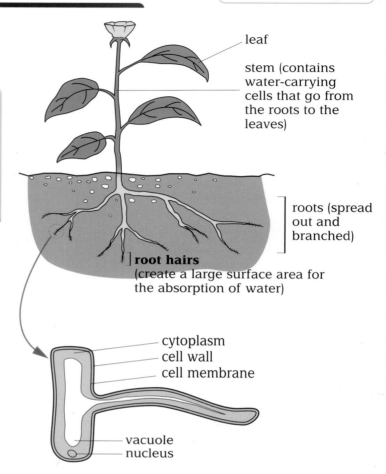

leaf

stem (contains water-carrying cells that go from the roots to the leaves)

roots (spread out and branched)

root hairs (create a large surface area for the absorption of water)

cytoplasm
cell wall
cell membrane

vacuole
nucleus

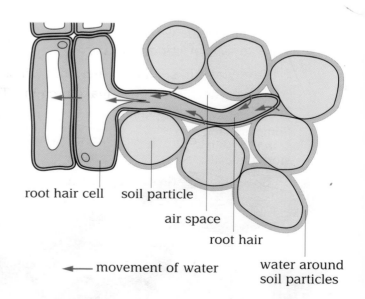

root hair cell   soil particle

air space

root hair

← movement of water

water around soil particles

A root hair cell in the soil

How plants use water

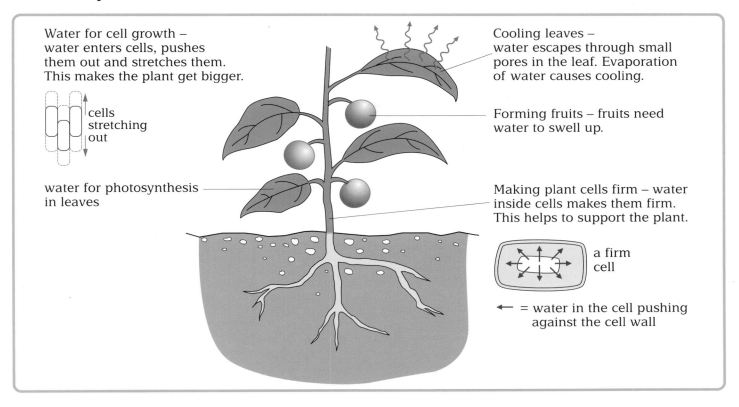

Water for cell growth – water enters cells, pushes them out and stretches them. This makes the plant get bigger.

cells stretching out

water for photosynthesis in leaves

Cooling leaves – water escapes through small pores in the leaf. Evaporation of water causes cooling.

Forming fruits – fruits need water to swell up.

Making plant cells firm – water inside cells makes them firm. This helps to support the plant.

a firm cell

← = water in the cell pushing against the cell wall

8 Use the information in the diagram to draw a table. Use the following headings in your table:
   ● **Use of water**
   ● **How does it happen?**

The use of minerals in plants

The water in soil has **minerals**, such as **nitrates**, dissolved in it. Plants need nitrates to make proteins. They need proteins to make and repair cells.

Look at the pictures of plants growing in solutions of minerals.

9 The experiment was set up to find out the effects of a lack of nitrate. Why was bottle A needed?

10 Explain why you need to set up 10 plants like this in each solution, not just the one of each shown.

11 Describe and explain the effects of a lack of nitrate on the plant.

12 Find out how farmers get extra minerals into the soil for their crops.

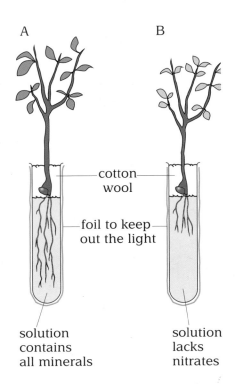

A   B

cotton wool

foil to keep out the light

solution contains all minerals

solution lacks nitrates

9C.5 Green plants and the environment

Millions of years ago, there was no oxygen in the Earth's atmosphere. Then green plants began to add oxygen. Now, the amounts of oxygen and carbon dioxide remain more or less balanced. Oxygen makes up about 21% of the atmosphere and carbon dioxide about 0.03%.

When they photosynthesise, all green plants take in carbon dioxide from the air and give out oxygen. Because of their large numbers, plants in tropical rainforests and oceans produce most of the oxygen. They also remove carbon dioxide from the air.

Look at the equations.

Photosynthesis: **energy**

carbon dioxide + water $\longrightarrow$ sugar + oxygen

Respiration:

sugar + oxygen $\longrightarrow$ carbon dioxide + water + energy

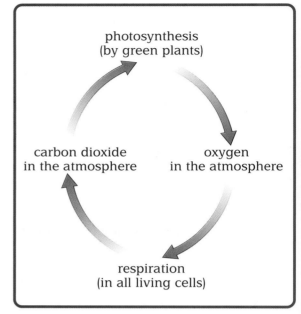

 1 Make a list of differences between the equations.

Altering the balance

As more forests are cut down, less carbon dioxide is removed from the atmosphere by plants. Also, the burning and rotting of wood increases the amount of carbon dioxide in the atmosphere.

 2 How much did the amount of carbon dioxide in the atmosphere increase between 1960 and 1990?

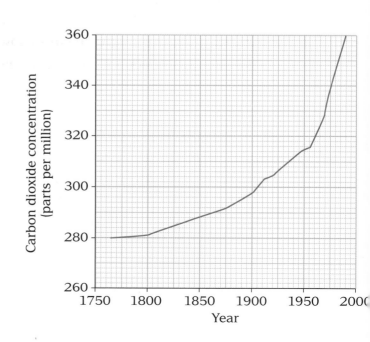

Carbon dioxide is one of a number of gases called greenhouse gases. Greenhouse gases stop heat escaping into space. Many scientists believe that this trapped heat is causing the planet to warm up. This is called global warming.

3 Find out the name of <u>one</u> other greenhouse gas.

Over millions of years, the temperature of our planet has often changed. Also, pollution that causes acid rain has a cooling effect on the planet.

4 Why has it been so difficult to say whether humans are causing global warming?

5 What types of evidence are scientists using to work out a link between global warming and what humans are doing?

Conservation is the protection of the environment. Conserving the forests of the world has many advantages.

- It helps to maintain the balance of gases in the atmosphere. This protects us from climate change.

- Forests provide timber, fruits, nuts, medicines and rubber.

- Forests provide a home for many living things.

6 Find out:

    a the name of a place in the world where people are cutting down forests;

    b why they are cutting the trees down there;

    c what the effects on their environment are.

You should now understand these key words and key ideas.

- Plants make food in their leaves by **photosynthesis**.

- The raw materials for photosynthesis are carbon dioxide and water.

- The light **energy** needed for photosynthesis is trapped by **chlorophyll**.

- Chlorophyll is found in **chloroplasts** in green parts of leaves.

- A plant's **biomass** is the matter that it is made of.

- **Glucose** from photosynthesis is used to make **starch**, to release energy during **respiration** and to make new materials.

- Roots are branched and have **root hairs** to increase their surface area. They need oxygen to respire.

- Plants use their roots to take up water and **minerals** such as nitrates.

- Plants need **nitrates** to make proteins for making and repairing cells.

- A plant uses water to cool its leaves, to swell up fruits, to make its cells firm and to stretch its cells for growth.

- Most photosynthesis happens in the cells near the top of the leaf.

- Plants produce oxygen in photosynthesis.

- About 21% of the air today is oxygen and about 0.03% is carbon dioxide.

- Plants in oceans and forests help to maintain the balance of oxygen and carbon dioxide in the atmosphere.

- Respiration, rotting and burning release carbon dioxide.

Plants for food

In this unit we shall be learning more about where our food comes from and some of the things that affect how much food we produce.

KEY WORDS
carnivore
herbivore
nutrients
fertilisers
yield
compete
weedkiller
pests
pesticide
herbicide
fungicide
insecticide
bioaccumulation
biodegradable
sustainable
  development

9D.1 Where does our food come from?

You learned in Unit 8A that your food supplies you with:

- energy for all your life processes;

- materials for growth and repair.

Only green plants <u>make</u> food. That is why we call them <u>producers</u>. Animals eat or consume food. So they are called <u>consumers</u>.

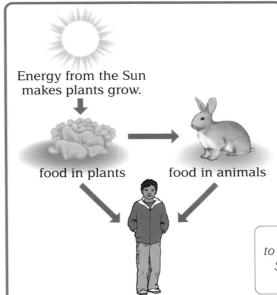

Energy from the Sun makes plants grow.

food in plants   food in animals

Plants use sunlight energy to make food in photosynthesis. So, the source of the <u>energy</u> in the food is the Sun.

1 Write down <u>two</u> examples of food from:
   a green plants;   **b** animals.

2 If it were not for the Sun and green plants, you'd have no food. Explain why.

3 Are you feeding as a primary consumer or a secondary consumer when you feed on:
   a green plants;
   b herbivores?

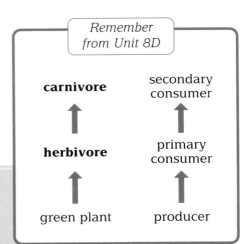

Remember from Unit 8D

carnivore   secondary consumer

↑   ↑

herbivore   primary consumer

↑   ↑

green plant   producer

Plants make glucose first; then they change some of it into other foods. Look at the diagram.

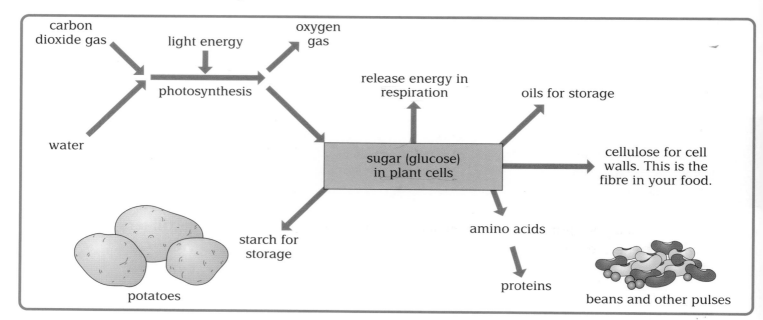

4 Plant cells use sugars in respiration.
Why do plant cells respire?

5 Why do plants make proteins?

A lot of our food is processed. Sometimes it is hard to tell which animals and plants it came from.

6 Look at the ingredients in the chicken pie.
Which ingredients come from:

a green plants? **b** animals?

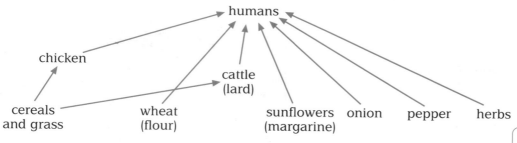

Ingredients

chicken	margarine
onion	herbs
flour	pepper
lard	salt

This food web shows where the ingredients in the chicken pie came from.

7 Draw a food web, like the one for the chicken pie, for your favourite meal.

Most of us don't grow or catch and kill our own food. Farmers in the UK and around the world grow the food we eat. As you saw in Unit 8A, people in different parts of the world often eat different things.

We eat different parts of different plants

Sometimes we can eat one part of a plant but not another.

In the food web for the chicken pie:

- flour, pepper and cooking oil come from seeds;

- onions are bulbs;

- herbs are usually leaves.

Some parts of plants are nicer to eat than others. Some contain more **nutrients** than others. Nutrients are materials, such as starches, oils and proteins, that <u>our</u> cells use. Like us, plants release energy from carbohydrates and fats in respiration. They store food so that they can survive the winter and grow new leaves in the spring. So we eat the food that plants make and store for their own benefit, not ours.

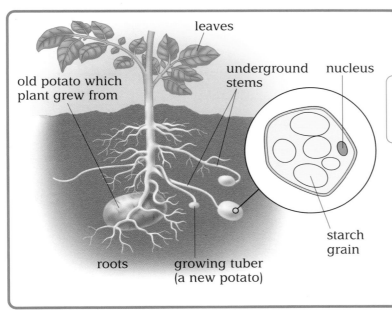

leaves

underground stems

nucleus

old potato which plant grew from

roots

growing tuber (a new potato)

starch grain

We eat potatoes, but the green parts of a potato plant are poisonous.

You can enjoy eating the apples, but not the bark or the leaves of an apple tree.

Look at the pictures.

8 Write down <u>two</u> reasons why we don't eat some parts of plants.

9 Write down:

    a <u>one</u> important nutrient that we get from potatoes;

    b <u>two</u> nutrients that we get from seeds.

10 Why do seeds contain proteins and an energy source?

11 The fleshy part of fruit, such as plums, contains sugars. The plum tree doesn't use these sugars in respiration. Animals eat and use them. Explain how the tree benefits from the sugars in plums.

	root	stem	leaves	leaf stalk	flower	fruit or seed
beans						●
broccoli					●	
cabbage			●			
carrot	●					
celery				●		
rice						●
sugar cane		●				
tomato						●
wheat						●

12 The table shows some parts of plants that we eat. Draw a similar table for the following foods.

    apple   coconut   grape   lettuce   maize   pea

    mango   onion   potato   radish   soya bean

Fruits and seeds contain proteins for growth and carbohydrate or fats for energy. When humans and other animals carry away and eat the soft, sugary parts of fruits, they are helping to spread the seeds that are inside the fruits.

9D.2 How do fertilisers affect plant growth?

The equation shows the raw materials and the products of photosynthesis.

energy from sunlight

carbon dioxide + water ⟶ sugars + oxygen

To make proteins, plants use sugars and minerals such as nitrates too.

energy from respiration   energy from respiration

sugars + minerals ⟶ amino acids ⟶ proteins

Plants also need small amounts of minerals to make chlorophyll and other chemicals. So minerals are <u>plant nutrients</u> and plants take them into their roots from the soil.

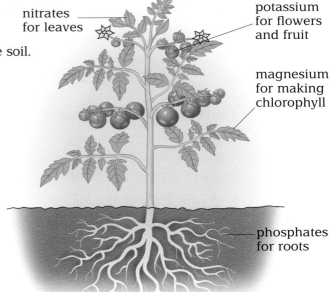

nitrates for leaves

potassium for flowers and fruit

magnesium for making chlorophyll

phosphates for roots

1   Write down <u>two</u> reasons why plants need minerals.

2   Write down the minerals that plants need for healthy growth of:

   a leaves;   **b** roots.

When farmers and gardeners harvest plants, they take away the minerals stored in them. So to make sure that the next crop gets enough minerals, they add **fertilisers** to the soil.

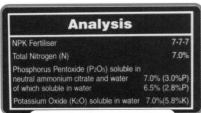

Analysis	
NPK Fertiliser	7-7-7
Total Nitrogen (N)	7.0%
Phosphorus Pentoxide (P_2O_5) soluble in neutral ammonium citrate and water	7.0% (3.0%P)
of which soluble in water	6.5% (2.8%P)
Potassium Oxide (K_2O) soluble in water	7.0%(5.8%K)

The fertiliser contains the minerals that plants use most.

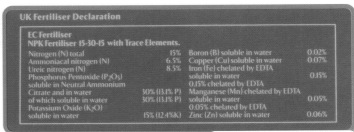

UK Fertiliser Declaration

EC Fertiliser
NPK Fertiliser 15-30-15 with Trace Elements.

Nitrogen (N) total	15%	Boron (B) soluble in water	0.02%
Ammoniacal nitrogen (N)	6.5%	Copper (Cu) soluble in water	0.07%
Ureic nitrogen (N)	8.5%	Iron (Fe) chelated by EDTA	
Phosphorus Pentoxide (P_2O_5) soluble in Neutral Ammonium		soluble in water	0.15%
		0.15% chelated by EDTA	
Citrate and in water	30% (13.1% P)	Manganese (Mn) chelated by EDTA	
of which soluble in water	30% (13.1% P)	soluble in water	0.05%
Potassium Oxide (K_2O)		0.05% chelated by EDTA	
soluble in water	15% (12.4%K)	Zinc (Zn) soluble in water	0.06%

This fertiliser contains extra minerals.

3   **a** Write down <u>three</u> minerals that both fertilisers supply.

   b Write down <u>three</u> extra minerals in the second fertiliser.

4   Write down <u>two</u> things that you think farmers and gardeners take into account when they choose a fertiliser.

Lack of a mineral

We can investigate the lack of a particular mineral by putting small plants in water or clean sand that contains no minerals. Then we can add different minerals to find out what effects they have on plant growth.

Helen and Vijay grew 20 cuttings in sand. They gave 10 plants a fertiliser containing all the minerals that plants need. For a second group of 10 plants, they left out just one mineral. Plants A and B in the pictures are average plants from the two groups.

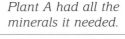
Plant A had all the minerals it needed.

Plant B lacked magnesium.

5 Why did Helen and Vijay grow their plants in sand?

6 Explain why they used 20 plants, rather than just two.

7 Suggest <u>two</u> other ways to make Helen and Vijay's test fair.

8 What do you think plants use magnesium for? Explain your answer.

Concentration of a mineral

We can find out how different concentrations of a mineral affect the **yield** of a crop. The yield is the amount of a crop that we can harvest.

Some students at an agricultural college used different amounts of nitrate fertiliser on wheat in different fields. They mixed different amounts of fertiliser with the same amount of water for each hectare. The graph shows their results.

Spreading fertiliser on a wheat crop.

9 Why do you think the students dissolved the different amounts of fertiliser in the same amount of water?

10 Describe what the students found out.

11 The highest yield of wheat was at 300 kg of fertiliser per hectare. But the students decided that using 200 kg per hectare was more sensible. Suggest a reason for this.

When you investigate fertilisers yourself, remember some of the ideas in this topic.

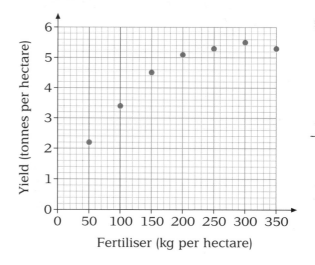

9D.3 Plants out of place

What is a weed?

A weed is a fast-growing plant that is growing where it is not wanted.

Couch grass in a flower border

Daisies in a lawn

1 In which photograph is the grass the weed?

2 In which photograph are the flowers the weed?

How do weeds affect crop production?

3 What do the roots of weeds and crops compete for?

4 What do the leaves of weeds and crops compete for?

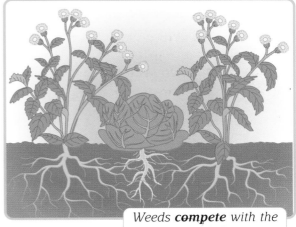

Weeds **compete** with the cabbage for light, water, minerals and space.

How do we control weeds?

Weeds can be removed by hand if crops are grown in rows that are far enough apart. This takes a lot of time and effort.

Farm workers weeding a field of strawberries.

A **weedkiller** is a chemical that kills weeds. You have to choose a weedkiller that doesn't kill your crop plants as well as the weeds. Look at the table.

Weedkiller	Action	Type of plant that it kills
Glyphosate	Plants wilt, leaves turn brown, then the plant dies.	All plants – leaves and roots
2,4-D	Causes unequal growth of leaf stalks and leaves. Leaves cup and twist as they grow, then the plant dies.	Broadleaved plants such as dandelion, plantain, daisy, clover and many crop plants
Diquat	Leaves turn yellow, then black.	Most plants, but not those with deep roots.

5   Which type of weedkiller would you use to get rid of couch grass? Couch grass has underground stems and deep roots that are very hard to kill.

6   Which weedkiller would you choose for getting rid of daisies in a lawn?

Farmers use selective weedkiller to kill broadleaved weeds in their wheat fields.

7   Why is it difficult to weed a field of wheat by hand?

8   Look at the pictures. Which field do farmers prefer?

9   Conservationists are people who want to preserve wild plants and animals. Which field do conservationists prefer?

10 Some weeds produce seeds that wild birds feed on. What will happen to the population of birds if farmers use weedkiller?

11 In a field of crops, nettles are weeds. But they are food for several animals. Find out what animals feed on nettles.

9D.4 Pests

These animals are **pests** because they eat farmers' crops, but they are also important food for other animals.

Some common pests of crop plants.

greenfly   slug   snail   mouse   cabbage white butterfly

Mrs Gilbert has a field of cabbages. Last year, her crop was badly damaged by slugs. This year, she has decided to use a **pesticide** to kill the slugs. She has chosen to use slug pellets – a pesticide that it is claimed kills only slugs and snails and is safe for other wildlife.

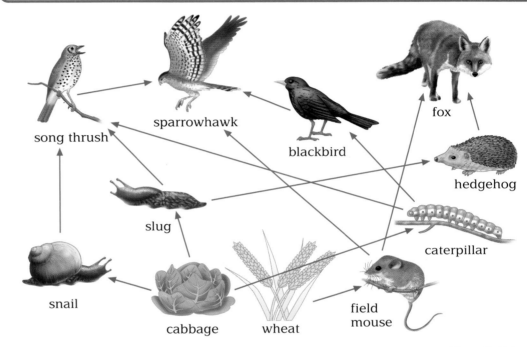

song thrush   sparrowhawk   blackbird   fox   hedgehog   slug   caterpillar   snail   cabbage   wheat   field mouse

A food web in Mrs Gilbert's cabbage field.

1 Caterpillars are usually treated as pests by humans, but name <u>two</u> animals which find caterpillars useful.

2 Look at the food web and describe how you think using slug pellets will affect the population of:

   a snails;   **b** song thrushes;   **c** sparrowhawks.

3 If slugs and snails are killed, the cabbage white caterpillar population will change. Explain why the caterpillar population might go:

   a up;   **b** down.

4 How can you explain to Mrs Gilbert that, even if the claim that slug pellets kill only snails and slugs is true, other wildlife will still be affected?

5 Find out if slug pellets really are safe for other wildlife.

What are pesticides?

Pests can damage up to 40% of a crop. Farmers use pesticides so that they can produce:

- more food and make more profit;
- undamaged food, which will sell for a good price.

Pesticides kill other wildlife as well as pests.

Type of pesticide	What it kills
Herbicide	Plants
Fungicide	Fungi
Insecticide	Insects

6 Farmers don't spray their crops with insecticide when the crops are flowering. Why do you think this is?

7 What do you think '-cide' means at the end of a word?

8 Make up a name for a pesticide that kills <u>rodents</u> such as rats and mice.

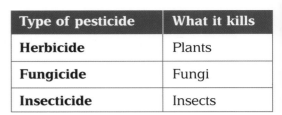

Not all insects are pests of crop plants. Useful insects, such as bees, pollinate flowers.

Persistent pesticides

Some pesticides aren't broken down easily in the body or in the environment. We call these persistent pesticides. DDT is an example of a persistent pesticide that is now banned in Europe and many other parts of the world.

1 DDT is sprayed onto fields at a safe dose for wildlife. Some is washed into streams and is absorbed by tiny water plants and animals.

4 A heron eats hundreds of fish, so it could accumulate a toxic amount of DDT – enough to kill it.

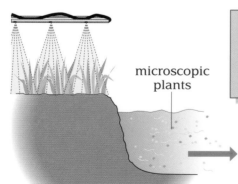

microscopic plants

2 Small fish eat the tiny plants and animals and the DDT is stored in their bodies.

3 Even more builds up in larger fish. We call this **bioaccumulation**.

9 Look at the diagram. How did DDT kill herons when it was sprayed on crops in a dilute 'safe' amount?

10 Why do you think it was 10 years before scientists realised there was a problem with DDT?

Non-persistent pesticides

Pyrethroids are non-persistent pesticides; they break down into simpler substances in living cells and in the environment. We say that they are **biodegradable**.

11 Why do farmers now use non-persistent pesticides? Explain as fully as you can.

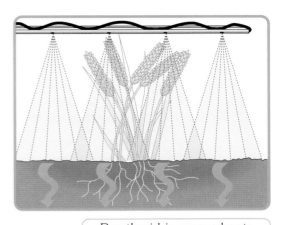

Pyrethroid is sprayed onto fields at a safe dose for wildlife. It breaks down quickly into harmless chemicals once it reaches the soil and is no longer toxic.

9D.5 Producing more food

How the environment affects plant growth

The diagram summarises what you should know about the effects of the environment on plants.

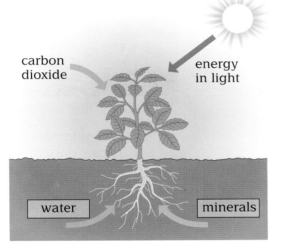

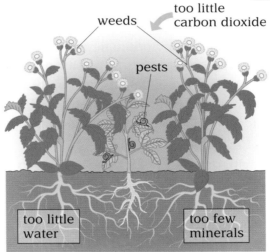

1 Write down <u>five</u> environmental conditions that affect plant growth.

2 **a** Write down <u>two</u> forms of energy that plants need for growth.

b Where does this energy usually come from?

Improving the environment for plants

Farmers and gardeners control some environmental conditions for their plants. They can buy fertilisers or grow plants in heated greenhouses, but it is too expensive to control everything.

3 Look at the diagram again. Write a list of substances that farmers might need to add to make their crops grow faster.

Some environments provide better conditions for plants than others, and the better the conditions, the higher the yield of a crop. So farmers in different places supply different things.

4 Why are outdoor crops larger and faster growing in Malaysia than in:

    a Egypt;   **b** the UK?

5 Tomato growers in the UK heat their greenhouses. Write down <u>one</u> benefit and <u>one</u> disadvantage of doing this.

6 In the UK, crops such as wheat and beans grow faster in higher temperatures. Why don't we provide higher temperatures for them?

7 Find out some benefits and some disadvantages of growing crops in greenhouses.

Can we produce more food?

As well as controlling the environment, farmers and scientists use selective breeding and other ways of producing plants that give better crops. You came across this idea in Unit 9A. But scientists think that the population of Earth will double by the year 2050. So even more food will be needed by then.

8 Compared with growing fodder barley in open fields, explain why fodder units:

    a produce fodder more quickly;

    b use much less water.

One problem is that in other places good land is being destroyed by overuse. What we need are ways of continuing to produce more food without damaging the Earth. This will let development continue, so we call it **sustainable development**.

9 Write down <u>two</u> reasons why we need scientists to carry on researching crops and crop production.

In Malaysia, the climate is wet, hot and sunny. Farmers use manure as a fertiliser and need to control pests, weeds and diseases.

Egypt is dry, hot and sunny. Salim uses manure to provide plant nutrients, takes out weeds and sometimes uses pesticides. He pumps water into channels in his fields daily. We call this <u>irrigation</u>.

Some farmers use fodder units to grow barley 'grass' from seed. It takes 2 or 3 litres of water to produce each kilogram of fodder. Solar oanels provide heat and light.

In commercial greenhouses in the UK, growers control pests and diseases and the amounts of water and fertilisers. Opening and closing of windows is automatic.

You should now understand these key words and key ideas.

KEY WORDS
carnivore
herbivore
nutrients
fertilisers
yield
compete
weedkiller
pests
pesticide
herbicide
fungicide
insecticide
bioaccumulation
biodegradable
sustainable
  development

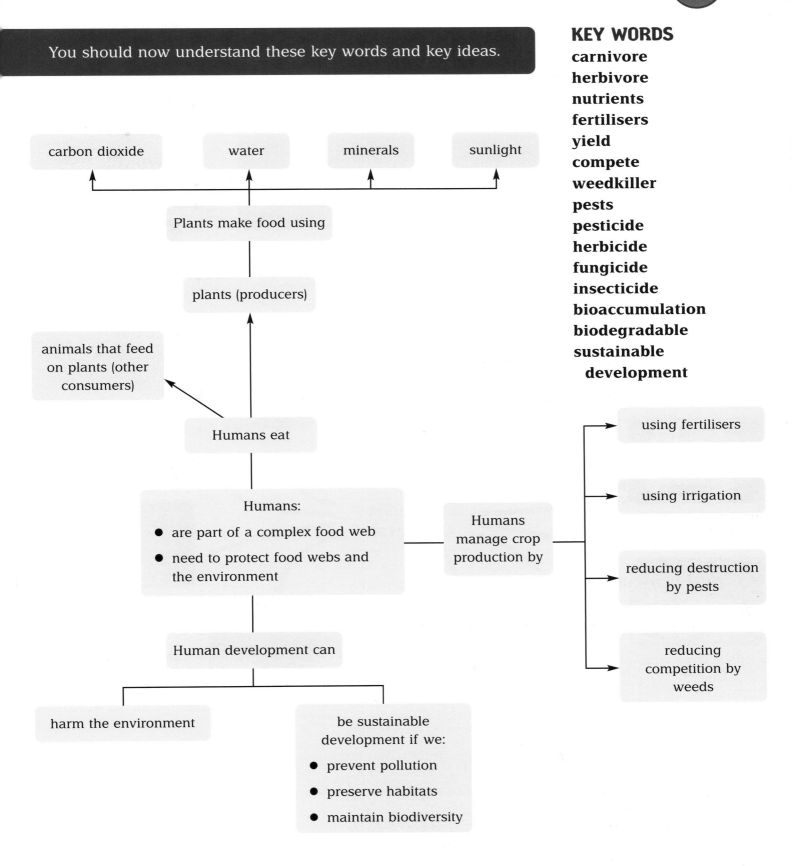

carbon dioxide water minerals sunlight

Plants make food using

plants (producers)

animals that feed on plants (other consumers)

Humans eat

Humans:
● are part of a complex food web
● need to protect food webs and the environment

Humans manage crop production by

using fertilisers

using irrigation

reducing destruction by pests

reducing competition by weeds

Human development can

harm the environment

be sustainable development if we:
● prevent pollution
● preserve habitats
● maintain biodiversity

Reactions of metals and metal compounds

In this unit we shall be learning about the properties of metals and their compounds. We shall also explore how metals and metal compounds react with acids.

KEY WORDS
metal
property
physical property
chemical property
non-metal
metal carbonate
ores
metal oxide

9E.1 Why are metals useful?

Although **metals** vary, they all have some things in common. These things are called the **properties** of metals.

have high melting points so are solid at room temperature

are shiny when polished

are dense

are good conductors of electricity

Properties of metals

can be hammered and bent into shape; are usually tough and strong

are good conductors of heat

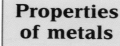
have alkaline oxides

form mixtures of metals called alloys

only three metals are magnetic, iron, nickel and cobalt

The properties of metals

1   Write down six properties that all metals have in common.

2   What property makes iron, cobalt and nickel special?

Although metals have properties in common, there is variation between them. That is why we use different metals for different jobs.

3 Explain why we use copper for pipes and wiring in our homes.

4 Explain how particular properties of aluminium determine its uses.

5 Explain why gold jewellery stays shiny for a long time.

6 Explain why iron is used to make cooking pans.

Aluminium, Al
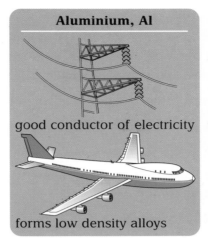
good conductor of electricity

forms low density alloys

Copper, Cu
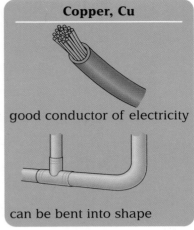
good conductor of electricity

can be bent into shape

Gold, Au

unreactive, so stays shiny for a long time

Iron, Fe
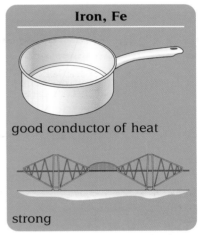
good conductor of heat

strong

Some uses of metals

Properties of non-metals

You could say that **non-metals** have the opposite properties to metals.

Properties of metals	Properties of non-metals
have high melting points	have low melting and boiling points
are shiny	are dull
can be hammered and bent into shape	are usually brittle when solid
are good conductors of heat	are poor conductors of heat (are insulators)
are good conductors of electricity	are poor conductors of electricity (are insulators)
form alloys	do not form alloys
iron, nickel and cobalt are magnetic	no non-metals are magnetic

7 What name is given to a substance that does not let electricity pass through it?

8 What name is given to a substance that does not let heat pass through it?

Metal or non-metal?

Once you have found out its properties, it is usually easy to work out if an element is a metal or a non-metal. However, you need to be careful! Some metals and non-metals have unexpected properties:

- Mercury is a metal that is a liquid at room temperature.

- Graphite (a form of carbon) is a non-metal that is a good conductor of electricity.

- Diamond (another form of carbon) is a non-metal that is the hardest known natural substance.

When you are trying to decide if an element is a metal or a non-metal, you need to look at more than one property.

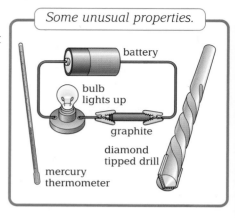

Some unusual properties.

Property	Element X
appearance	shiny, dark-grey solid
melting point	1410 °C
electrical conductivity	medium
thermal (heat) conductivity	low

 9 Name a non-metal that conducts electricity.

 10 What property of mercury enables it to be used in thermometers?

 11 Look at the table. Is element X a metal or a non-metal? Explain your answer.

Physical and chemical properties

The properties that we have looked at so far describe what an element is like. These are its **physical properties**. An element's **chemical properties** describe how it reacts. The pictures shown an example.

 12 Does calcium oxide form acidic or alkaline solutions?

 13 Some sulphur dioxide is dissolved in water to form a solution. What is the pH of this solution?

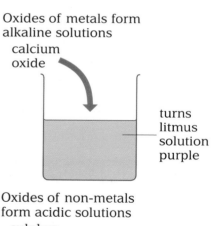

Oxides of metals form alkaline solutions
calcium oxide

turns litmus solution purple

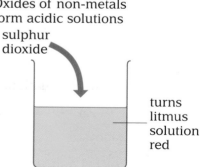

Oxides of non-metals form acidic solutions
sulphur dioxide

turns litmus solution red

9E.2 Reacting metals with acids

We have seen that metals vary. Particular combinations of properties make different metals suitable for different jobs. It would be no use making a saucepan out of a metal that then explodes when it is heated up or reacts when you put water in it!

Metals and acids

Look at the pictures and the table.

Name of acid	Formula
hydrochloric acid	HCl
sulphuric acid	H_2SO_4

1 What is the evidence in the pictures for chemical reactions?

2 Describe the test for hydrogen. (Remember from Unit 7F.)

Hydrogen is not the only product of reactions between metals and acids. Salts are always produced. Look at the picture.

What we need to do now is name the salt. We can do this by writing word and symbol equations for what we know about the reaction:

zinc + sulphuric acid → hydrogen + ...

$Zn + H_2SO_4 → H_2 + ...$

There is no Zn or SO_4 on the right-hand side of the equation. The Zn and the SO_4 join together to make the salt, $ZnSO_4$, called zinc sulphate.

word equation:

zinc + sulphuric acid → zinc sulphate + hydrogen

symbol equation:

$Zn + H_2SO_4 → ZnSO_4 + H_2$

3 What is the name of the salt produced when zinc reacts with sulphuric acid?

4 Name the elements found in sulphuric acid.

zinc reacting with...

hydrochloric acid

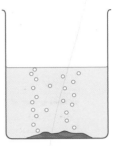

sulphuric acid

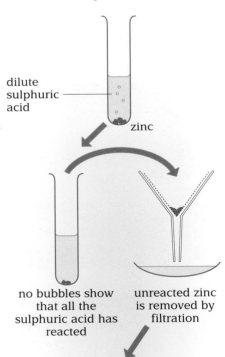

dilute sulphuric acid

zinc

no bubbles show that all the sulphuric acid has reacted

unreacted zinc is removed by filtration

water evaporated from the solution

heat

crystals of salt are left

Getting the salt

Metals and acids – word equations

We know that most metals react with acids in a similar way. The general word equation is:

metal + acid → salt + hydrogen

All we have to work out is the name of the salt formed in the reaction. This is done by taking the name of metal and adding the name of the acid to it.

Name of acid	Name of salt produced
sulphuric acid	sulphate
hydrochloric acid	chloride
nitric acid	nitrate

We can now work out the name of the salt using the names of the metal and the acid. For example:

zinc + sulphuric acid → zinc sulphate + hydrogen

calcium + hydrochloric acid → calcium chloride + hydrogen

magnesium + nitric acid → magnesium nitrate + hydrogen

5   Name the salt formed when:

   a potassium reacts with sulphuric acid;

   b magnesium reacts with hydrochloric acid.

6   What acid would you use to make:

   a iron chloride and hydrogen from iron;

   b calcium nitrate and hydrogen from calcium?

7   Describe how you would prove that a salt forms when magnesium reacts with dilute hydrochloric acid.

9E.3 Reacting metal carbonates with acids

In chemistry we find there are several 'groups' of atoms which are often found together in chemical compounds. Nitrates, sulphates and carbonates are examples. We are going to explore how **metal carbonates** react with acids. Metal carbonates are chemical compounds made from a metal and the carbonate group, CO_3.

1 Name the elements found in calcium carbonate.

At the end of the reaction in the pictures a blue solution is formed. This is a salt called copper sulphate.

2 Look at the pictures. Write down <u>three</u> signs that a chemical reaction is happening.

3 The gas produced turns limewater milky white. Name the gas.

4 The symbol equation for this reaction is:

$$CuCO_3 + H_2SO_4 \longrightarrow CuSO_4 + H_2O + CO_2$$

Write the word equation.

All metal carbonates react with acids in a similar way. The chemical reaction between a metal carbonate and an acid always produces a salt, water and carbon dioxide. We can write a general word equation:

metal carbonate + acid → salt + water + carbon dioxide

5 Which gas is always produced when a metal carbonate reacts with an acid?

6 Name the salt formed when:

   a iron carbonate reacts with sulphuric acid;

   b magnesium carbonate reacts with nitric acid.

7 What reactants would you use to make:

   a iron chloride, water and carbon dioxide;

   b magnesium sulphate, water and carbon dioxide?

Copper carbonate and dilute sulphuric acid react to form copper sulphate.

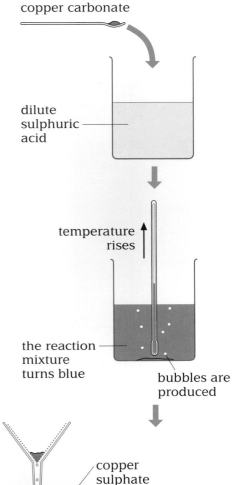

copper carbonate

dilute sulphuric acid

temperature rises

the reaction mixture turns blue

bubbles are produced

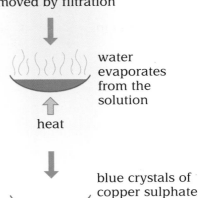

copper sulphate solution

once the reaction stops bubbling, the unreacted copper carbonate is removed by filtration

water evaporates from the solution

heat

blue crystals of copper sulphate are left

9E.4 Reacting metal oxides with acids

Many metal **ores** are oxides.

Name of metal oxide	Formula
copper oxide	CuO
sodium oxide	Na$_2$O
zinc oxide	ZnO

1 Name the element which is found in all metal oxides.

The diagrams show the reaction between copper oxide and dilute sulphuric acid.

2 Describe how you can see that the copper oxide has reacted with the dilute sulphuric acid.

3 What method of separation is used to remove unreacted copper oxide from the solution?

The word equation for the reaction shown is:

copper oxide + sulphuric acid → copper sulphate + water

The symbol equation is:

$$CuO + H_2SO_4 \rightarrow CuSO_4 + H_2O$$

4 Why were there no bubbles in this reaction?

All **metal oxides** react with acids in a similar way. The chemical reaction between a metal oxide and an acid always produces a salt and water, so we can write a general word equation:

metal oxide + acid → salt + water

We can now predict what is made in the chemical reaction between any metal oxide and any acid.

5 Name the products of a reaction between a metal oxide and an acid.

6 Name the salt formed when:

   a zinc oxide reacts with sulphuric acid;

   b iron oxide reacts with hydrochloric acid.

7 What reactants would you use to make:

   a copper chloride and water;

   b magnesium sulphate and water?

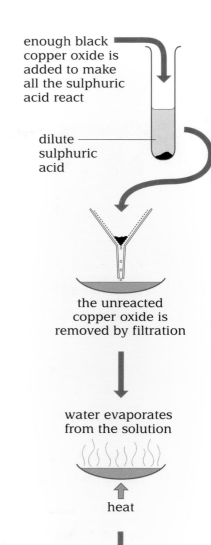

enough black copper oxide is added to make all the sulphuric acid react

dilute sulphuric acid

the unreacted copper oxide is removed by filtration

water evaporates from the solution

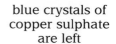

heat

blue crystals of copper sulphate are left

9E.5 More about salts

The first part of the name of a salt comes from a metal and the second part comes from an acid.

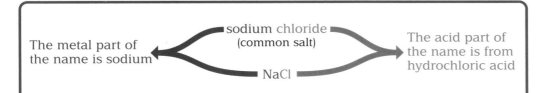

The metal part of the name is sodium ← sodium chloride (common salt) / NaCl → The acid part of the name is from hydrochloric acid

Name of salt	Formula
copper sulphate	$CuSO_4$
sodium chloride	$NaCl$
zinc nitrate	$Zn(NO_3)_2$

Salts have many different uses.

gunpowder contains potassium nitrate

copper sulphate, used as a fungicide in agriculture

Epsom salts are magnesium sulphate

photographic film contains silver nitrate

1 What is the chemical name for 'common salt'?

2 What is <u>one</u> use of potassium nitrate?

Neutralisation reactions

In this unit we have seen three different reactions which produce salts:

- metal + acid
- metal carbonate + acid
- metal oxide + acid

In Unit 7E we used neutralisation reactions to make salts too.

Calamine lotion neutralises the acid in bee stings.

Indigestion tablets neutralise excess stomach acid.

Calcium carbonate neutralises acidic rainwater and soil.

3 Describe <u>one</u> everyday use of a neutralisation reaction.

4 Why is the treatment for bee stings alkaline?

We can make common salt in a neutralisation reaction.
This is the symbol equation:

$$HCl + NaOH \rightarrow NaCl + H_2O$$

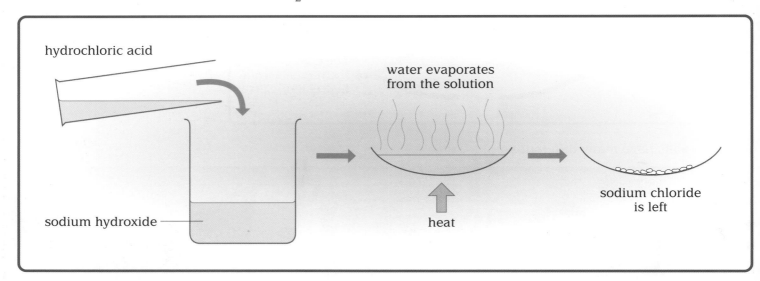

hydrochloric acid

water evaporates
from the solution

sodium hydroxide

heat

sodium chloride
is left

5 Name the type of reaction that happens between dilute
hydrochloric acid and sodium hydroxide solution.

6 **a** Write a word equation for the reaction between
hydrochloric acid and sodium hydroxide.

b Why don't we see bubbles in this reaction?

7 Name the salt formed when:

a magnesium hydroxide reacts with sulphuric acid;

b potassium hydroxide reacts with nitric acid.

8 What reactants would you use to make:

a calcium chloride and water;

b sodium sulphate and water?

When we use alkalis in chemical reactions we must make sure we
check their bottles for hazard warning signs. Just like acids, some
alkalis can be dangerous to use. Solutions of alkalis such as
calcium hydroxide are irritants and can cause your skin to
redden, blister and itch. Alkalis such as sodium hydroxide are
corrosive and will attack your skin and start eating it away.

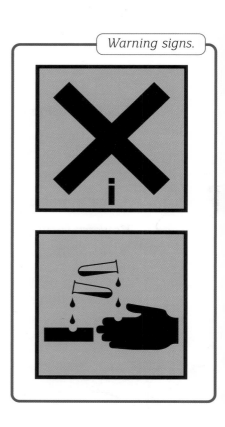

Warning signs.

Neutralisation – an ending

When neutralisation reactions are used in industry it is important that the correct amounts of acid and alkali are used. A product that is acidic or alkaline, when it should be neutral, is not much use. We are going to explore how we find out how much alkali is needed to neutralise an acid.

In Unit 7E you learned that a neutral solution has a pH of 7 and that you can measure it using universal indicator. We need to find out the volumes of acid and alkali to mix to form a solution of pH 7. We shall use potassium hydroxide, an alkali, and hydrochloric acid.

9 What is the pH of a neutral solution?

10 What colour does universal indicator turn in a neutral solution?

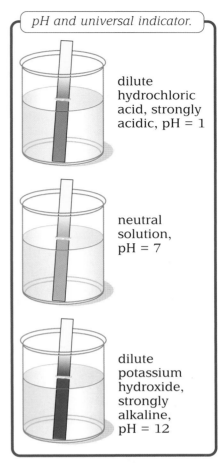

pH and universal indicator.

dilute hydrochloric acid, strongly acidic, pH = 1

neutral solution, pH = 7

dilute potassium hydroxide, strongly alkaline, pH = 12

Producing a neutral solution

A simple way of producing a neutral solution is to add the potassium hydroxide solution to the dilute hydrochloric acid until the universal indicator turns green. Adding it slowly enough is tricky. One way is to add the potassium hydroxide solution using a dropping pipette.

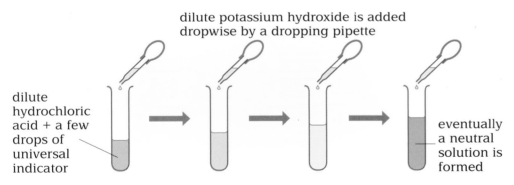

dilute potassium hydroxide is added dropwise by a dropping pipette

dilute hydrochloric acid + a few drops of universal indicator

eventually a neutral solution is formed

However, using a dropping pipette makes it very difficult to measure the exact volume of potassium hydroxide required for the neutralisation. Chemists use a piece of equipment called a burette. It allows them to add the potassium hydroxide solution slowly in precise amounts and to measure the volume accurately.

11 What piece of apparatus do chemists use to measure the exact volume of alkali added to an acid to produce a neutral solution?

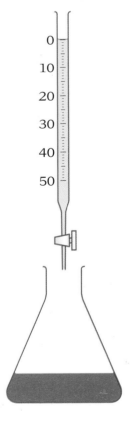

12 Why must the potassium hydroxide solution be added slowly?

13 What happens to the colour of the universal indicator when too much potassium hydroxide solution is added to the dilute hydrochloric acid?

Finding the exact volume

An alternative way is to add the potassium hydroxide solution to the dilute hydrochloric acid 1 cm³ at a time. After each addition of potassium hydroxide solution the mixture is swirled and its pH written down. The pH can be found using universal indicator and a pH card. Alternatively a digital device called a pH probe can be used to get a really accurate measure of the pH. The results of such an experiment are given in the table.

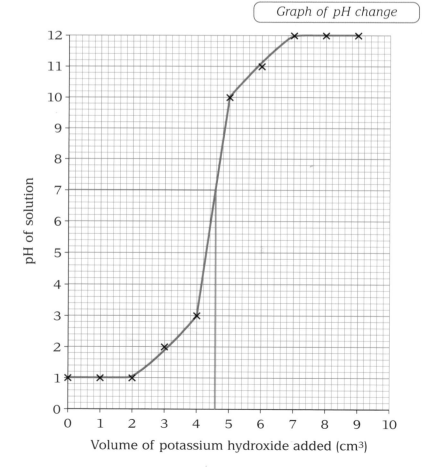

Using a pH probe

Volume of potassium hydroxide added (cm³)	0	1	2	3	4	5	6	7	8	9
pH of solution	1	1	1	2	3	10	11	12	12	12

The results of this experiment can be plotted as a graph. The graph clearly shows how the pH changes during the neutralisation reaction. A neutral solution is produced when the pH reaches exactly 7. We can use the graph to find out how much potassium hydroxide must be added to the dilute hydrochloric acid to get a solution of exactly pH 7.

Graph of pH change

14 Write down <u>two</u> ways of measuring the pH of a mixture of potassium hydroxide solution and dilute hydrochloric acid.

15 Use the graph to find the exact volume of potassium hydroxide solution needed to neutralise the hydrochloric acid.

You should now understand the key words and key ideas shown below.

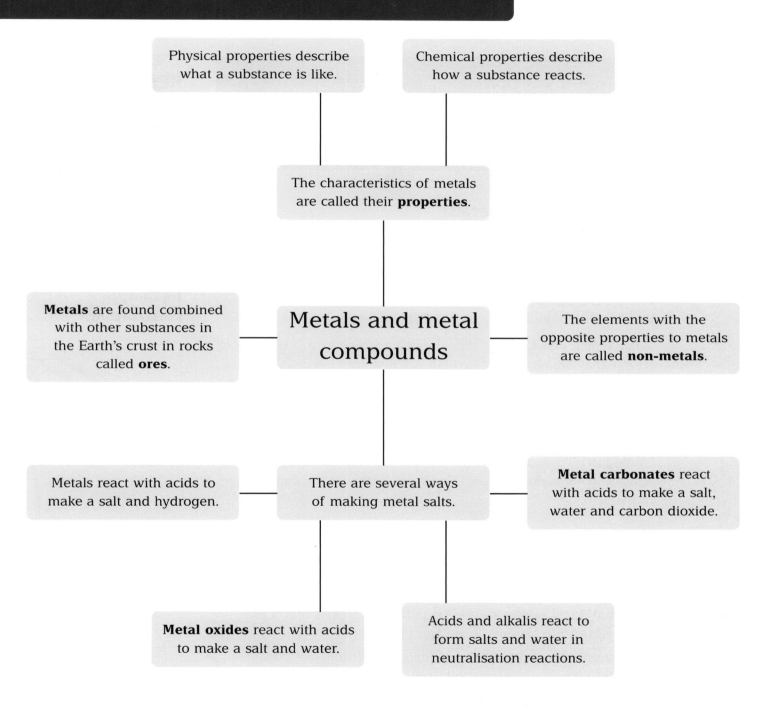

Physical properties describe what a substance is like.

Chemical properties describe how a substance reacts.

The characteristics of metals are called their **properties**.

Metals are found combined with other substances in the Earth's crust in rocks called **ores**.

Metals and metal compounds

The elements with the opposite properties to metals are called **non-metals**.

Metals react with acids to make a salt and hydrogen.

There are several ways of making metal salts.

Metal carbonates react with acids to make a salt, water and carbon dioxide.

Metal oxides react with acids to make a salt and water.

Acids and alkalis react to form salts and water in neutralisation reactions.

Patterns of reactivity

In this unit we shall investigate some reactions of metals and compare their reactivity so that we can put them into a reactivity series. Then we shall use the reactivity series to make predictions about how some metals may react.

KEY WORDS
tarnish
alkali metal
reactivity
reactivity series
predict
salt
displacement reactions
displace
ore
haematite
electrolysis

9F.1 What happens to metals?

Some metals are more reactive than others. When they react with water or other substances in the environment, they change their appearance. We use the metal gold for jewellery because it doesn't change, even over a long period of time. Most other metals don't remain shiny for very long.

When metals change their appearance from a shiny to a dull colour we say they are tarnished. **Tarnish** is a discoloration caused by the reaction between the metal and oxygen. It is an oxidation reaction – a chemical reaction between the metal and its environment. Washing and polishing can remove tarnish, but if you leave any detergent or polish on the surface of the metal, it attracts moisture, leading to a far worse problem – corrosion. Tarnish is not damaging – it is not dirt, and it does not penetrate the surface of metal.

1   Name <u>one</u> metal which does not tarnish easily.

2   What do you think are the properties of copper that make it particularly useful for making pipes?

3   Joy wants to make some jewellery out of iron, but Dan thinks that it would not sell very well. Suggest why iron jewellery is not likely to sell.

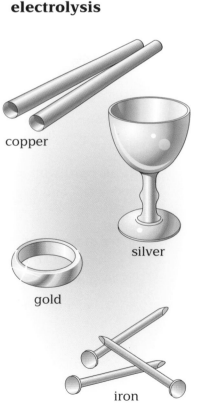

copper

silver

gold

iron

Four different metals.

Metals such as lithium, sodium and potassium tarnish very quickly. A newly cut surface is very shiny, but if you leave the surface exposed it quickly changes to become a dull grey colour.

4 How can you prove that sodium is really a metal?

5 How does the oil protect the metal from tarnishing?

Storing metals such as sodium in oil protects them from tarnishing.

9F.2 Metals and water

Sodium is very reactive with water. When we add a small piece to water it fizzes around the surface producing bubbles of a gas. In a similar reaction with potassium instead of sodium, the reaction produces enough heat for the gas to catch fire.

1 **a** What is the chemical formula of water?

b What is the chemical symbol for sodium?

The gas produced in this reaction could be oxygen or hydrogen, because both these elements are present in the compound water.

2 Joy thinks that the gas produced is hydrogen and not oxygen. What evidence is there from the experiment to support her idea?

Sodium reacting with water.

When a few drops of universal indicator were added to the liquid in the trough, the indicator turned purple.

3 What does the indicator tell you about the liquid in the beaker at the end of the experiment?

In this experiment the sodium has reacted with the water to produce two new substances. They are hydrogen (the flammable gas) and sodium hydroxide (the alkaline solution).

We can describe this reaction using a word equation:

sodium + water → sodium hydroxide + hydrogen

Sodium, potassium and lithium all produce an alkaline solution. So we call them the **alkali metals**.

4 Work out the word equations for the reaction of:

a potassium with water

b lithium with water.

We know that other metals are not as reactive with water as sodium is. In fact, some metals do not react with water, even after a long time. So these metals are useful for making objects to hold or carry water. Gold, silver and copper are examples.

 5 Give <u>four</u> examples of uses of metals, where the metal needs to be unreactive to water.

Between these extremes of reactivity there are a number of metals that are moderately reactive with water.

 6 Look at the pictures. Which do you think is the more reactive metal, calcium or magnesium?

Some metals, such as iron, zinc and aluminium, don't seem to react with water. They do react, but it takes a bit longer to see what is happening.

 7 If you leave an iron nail in water, what evidence will there be after a week that a chemical reaction has taken place?

We now have enough information to place the metals in a league table based on their **reactivity**. We call this league table the **reactivity series**. If we know their position in the reactivity series, we can use it to **predict** how other metals will behave.

 8 Nickel is a metal that is a little more reactive than copper but not as reactive as iron.

    a How will nickel behave when you put it in water?

    b Colette thinks we could use nickel to make coins. Do you agree? Explain your answer.

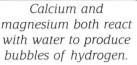

Calcium and magnesium both react with water to produce bubbles of hydrogen.

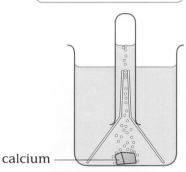

calcium

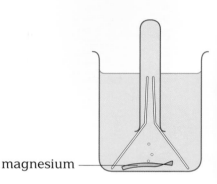

magnesium

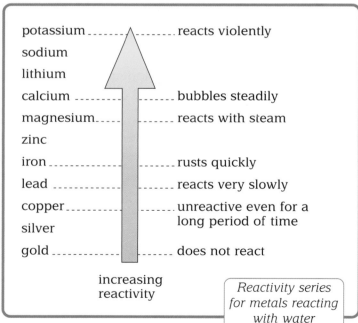

potassium	reacts violently
sodium	
lithium	
calcium	bubbles steadily
magnesium	reacts with steam
zinc	
iron	rusts quickly
lead	reacts very slowly
copper	unreactive even for a long period of time
silver	
gold	does not react

increasing reactivity

Reactivity series for metals reacting with water

9F.3 Reactivity of metals with acids

Only a few metals react quickly with water. The reaction between metals and acids is much more vigorous. When a metal does react with an acid, it is easy to see that a reaction is happening. Bubbles of gas are produced and the metal gradually disappears. The metal reacts with the acid to a form a new substance that is soluble in water. The gas produced is hydrogen and the other new substance is a **salt**. Most salts are soluble in water.

We can also look at the number of bubbles of hydrogen that are produced when reacting metals with cold or hot acid. Less reactive metals react only with hot acid.

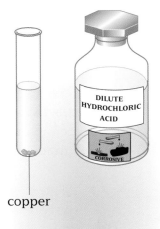

copper

 1 From the diagrams, what is the evidence that copper is more reactive than gold?

 2 Look at the diagrams at the bottom of the page. Which metal:

a reacts fastest with cold acid;

b reacts the most slowly with hot acid?

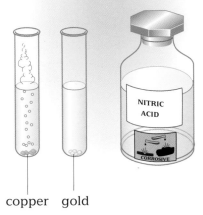

copper   gold

 3 Based on their reactions with cold acid and hot acid, place these four metals in order of reactivity.

4 Which metal is the most difficult to place in order? Explain your answer.

The reactivity series for the reactions between acids and metals is very similar to the one for water. But we get more detailed information because more metals react with acid than with water.

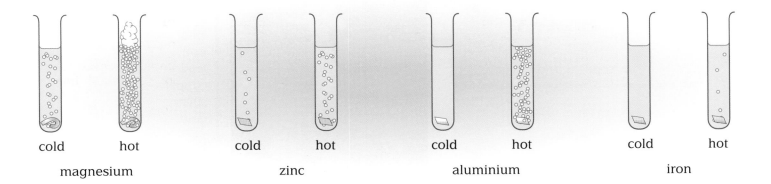

| cold | hot | cold | hot | cold | hot | cold | hot |
| magnesium | | zinc | | aluminium | | iron | |

9F.4 Metals and oxygen

The reaction between metals and oxygen is important because all the metals that we use every day are exposed to the oxygen in the atmosphere.

For example, steel is used to make cars, bridges and railway lines. Steel is made from iron, a moderately reactive metal. It reacts with oxygen to make iron oxide which is much weaker than iron. So the iron gradually reacts with oxygen and loses its strength.

1 Why do we not make bridges and cars out of gold, silver or copper? Give at least <u>two</u> reasons.

The word equation for the reaction between iron and oxygen is:

iron + oxygen → iron oxide

There is also water vapour in the atmosphere. Iron reacts with both water and oxygen to produce a substance called hydrated iron oxide. We usually call it 'rust'.

The word equation for rusting is:

iron + water + oxygen → hydrated iron oxide
(rust)

We protect iron objects such as cars and bridges against rusting by preventing oxygen and water from getting to the metal.

2 How do we protect bridges and cars from rusting?

3 Write word equations for the following reactions:

a copper and oxygen;

b magnesium and oxygen;

c sodium and oxygen.

One way to protect metals is to paint them.

Another way to protect metals is to oil them.

Magnesium burns very brightly.

potassium
sodium
lithium
calcium
magnesium
zinc
iron
lead
copper
silver
gold

increasing reactivity with oxygen

Again, we can make a reactivity series and use it to make predictions about other metals.

9F.5 Displacement reactions

Reactive metals tend not to remain as pure metals but to combine with other elements to form compounds.

As you have seen, the most reactive metals, such as potassium and sodium, react the most quickly.

When two metals are present, they compete to form new compounds. The more reactive metal will win the competition. We call a competition reaction a **displacement reaction**.

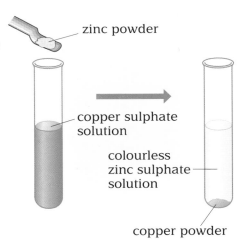

1 What evidence is there of a chemical reaction betweenthe zinc powder and the copper sulphate solution?

2 Describe the <u>two</u> products of the reaction between copper sulphate and zinc.

The word equation for this reaction is:

zinc + copper sulphate → zinc sulphate + copper
metal   solution   solution   metal

Copper sulphate and zinc sulphate are salts. Zinc is a more reactive metal than copper, so it **displaces** the copper from the copper sulphate and forms its own salt, zinc sulphate. The displaced copper is no longer part of a compound. It is an element – the orange/brown metal at the bottom of the test-tube.

3 Why does the liquid in the test-tube change from blue to colourless?

If you put a strip of copper metal into zinc sulphate solution, nothing happens. This is because the copper is the less reactive of the two and therefore cannot displace the zinc.

You can use the results of reactions between metals and solutions of metal salts to work out whether one metal is more reactive than another.

4 Look at the results of the experiments. In which of the experiments is there evidence of a chemical reaction?

5 Use these results to place the metals in an order of reactivity.

At the start	A few minutes later
copper tin nitrate	tin nitrate
copper magnesium nitrate	magnesium nitrate
tin copper nitrate	tin crystals
tin magnesium nitrate	magnesium nitrate
magnesium copper nitrate	copper crystals
magnesium tin nitrate	tin crystals

We can think of displacement reactions as a 'trial of strength' to see which metal will win the battle and become part of a salt rather than stay as a pure metal.

- Reactive metals, such as potassium and sodium, are really strong and will win most battles.

- Unreactive metals, such as copper and silver, are weak and usually lose their battles.

- Moderately reactive metals, such as iron or zinc, are somewhere in the middle and therefore they win some battles and lose others.

6   Which metal do you think will win the following battles, based on their position in the reactivity series?

a magnesium and iron

b gold and silver

c zinc and copper

d sodium and calcium

e zinc and iron

f potassium and sodium

A useful displacement reaction

In reactions between a metal and a metal oxide, the more reactive metal takes oxygen away from the less reactive metal. We say that it **displaces** the less reactive metal. The Thermit reaction uses this difference in reactivity between two metals, aluminium and iron. We use it to produce molten iron to repair railway lines on site. The Thermit mixture contains iron oxide and aluminium. When the mixture is heated, the more reactive aluminium takes the oxygen away from the iron oxide to produce pure iron. The heat given off in the reaction is so intense that it makes the iron melt.

The word equation for this reaction is:

iron oxide + aluminium → aluminium oxide + iron

7 Which of the substances in the equation are:

a elements;

b compounds?

8 When iron is mixed with aluminium oxide and then heated, there is no reaction. Explain why.

9 In which of the following mixtures will heating result in a chemical reaction?

- copper and magnesium oxide
- magnesium and copper oxide
- magnesium and iron oxide
- zinc and copper oxide
- zinc and magnesium oxide

9F.6 Sources and uses of metals

Only a few metals are found in their natural state. We call them 'native' metals. Examples are gold, silver and copper.

 1 Where are gold, silver and copper in the reactivity series?

Gold, silver and copper were the first metals people ever used because they were easy to extract from the ground. All people had to do was:

● separate the metal from the rocks around it

● heat up the metal until it melted

● mould the metal to form the shape they wanted.

Although these metals were better than the stone and wood that had been used before, they were not good enough for some jobs.

 2 Look at the cartoon. Suggest why copper and gold were not always the best metals for the job.

The search has been on ever since to find more useful metals, but that is not as easy as it sounds. Most metals are found chemically combined with other elements such as oxygen and sulphur. The rocks that contain these compounds are called **ores**. **Haematite** is an ore containing a compound of iron called iron oxide (Fe_2O_3).

 3 How do you think the metals in rocks ended up chemically joined to oxygen?

Rock salt is mostly sodium combined with chlorine.

Bauxite is an ore that we get aluminium from. It is mainly aluminium combined with oxygen.

Galena is an ore that we get lead from. It is mainly lead combined with sulphur.

Haematite is an ore that we get iron from. It is mainly iron combined with oxygen.

4   How many elements are present in the compound iron oxide?

5   What is the name of aluminium ore?

6   Which metal is found in rock salt?

7   What is the name of an ore from which we can extract lead?

Before we can use these metals, we have to extract them from their ores. In the case of the iron oxide, we need to separate the iron from the oxygen in the compound. About 3500 years ago, people discovered that they could extract iron from its ore by heating it with charcoal using a very hot flame. Heating with charcoal can be used to extract lead, zinc and tin too.

pot

charcoal and iron oxide

bellows

air for the charcoal

8   Look back at page 64. Where in the reactivity series are the metals that can be extracted using charcoal?

Nowadays we extract iron in a blast furnace. The diagram shows what happens.

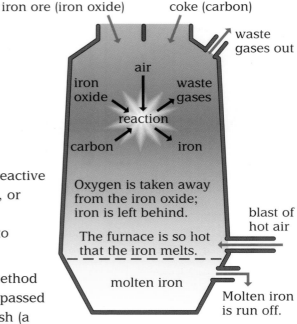

iron ore (iron oxide)   coke (carbon)

waste gases out

air

iron oxide   waste gases

reaction

carbon   iron

Oxygen is taken away from the iron oxide; iron is left behind.

The furnace is so hot that the iron melts.

blast of hot air

molten iron

Molten iron is run off.

9 What is blown into the blast furnace?

10 What is the source of the carbon?

11 How do you get the iron out of the blast furnace?

By 1800 only 12 metals were in common use. Only unreactive metals could be fairly extracted using carbon (charcoal), or hydrogen. More reactive metals, such as aluminium, magnesium and sodium, will not give up their oxygen to carbon or to hydrogen.

In 1807, the scientist Humphry Davy invented a new method of extracting very reactive metals. In an experiment he passed an electric current through a sample of moistened potash (a compound of potassium) on a platinum dish. He noticed that small globules of metal collected around the negative electrode. The metal that collected was potassium. He extracted sodium in a similar way.

This method of extracting metals by using an electric current is called **electrolysis**. Soon scientists found out how to use this method to extract metals such as calcium, barium, magnesium and aluminium. At first this method of extraction was very expensive. Napoleon III (1808–1873), the emperor of France, had a special dinner service made of aluminium which he used on special occasions to impress guests. Eventually the cost of these metals was reduced as scientists improved the methods of extraction. Aluminium is now a relatively cheap metal.

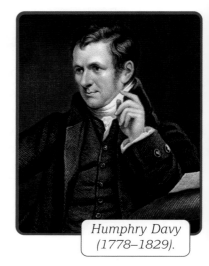

Humphry Davy (1778–1829).

Alloy	Metals in them
bronze	copper and tin
brass	copper and zinc
pewter	lead and tin
steel	iron and carbon

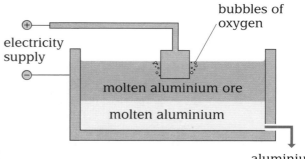

bubbles of oxygen

electricity supply

molten aluminium ore

molten aluminium

aluminium out

We extract aluminium by melting aluminium oxide and passing electricity through it.

12 What is aluminium oxide split up into?

13 Name <u>two</u> examples of household uses of aluminium which show that it must be relatively cheap.

By the end of the 19th century another 41 metals had been extracted from their ores. The Industrial Revolution depended on the availability of various metals that could do different jobs and could be produced economically. Look at the table.

Metal	Date of first extraction	Use
gold	6000 BC	jewellery
copper	4200 BC	electrical wiring
iron	1500 BC	railway lines
sodium	1807	street lighting
aluminium	1827	overhead cables

14 a Why is gold used for jewellery?

b Why can aluminium be used for overhead cables?

c Why can iron be used for railway lines?

9F.7 Investigating metals and acids further

Joy and Dan are investigating the reactivity of different metals with hydrochloric acid. When three of these metals react with acid, bubbles of gas are produced.

 1 What is the name of the gas produced?

The other product is a salt. When you use hydrochloric acid, the salt produced is always a chloride. So when magnesium reacts with hydrochloric acid, the salt produced is magnesium chloride.

 2 What are the products when aluminium reacts with hydrochloric acid?

Joy thinks that they can compare the reactivity of metals by looking at the number of bubbles produced when you add a strip of metal to some hydrochloric acid.

 3 What must Joy do to make sure this a fair test?
4 Look at the diagram. Then place the metals in an order of reactivity.

Two of the metals give very similar results. Joy decides that measuring the volume of gas produced would be more accurate than counting bubbles. She collects the gas in a burette.

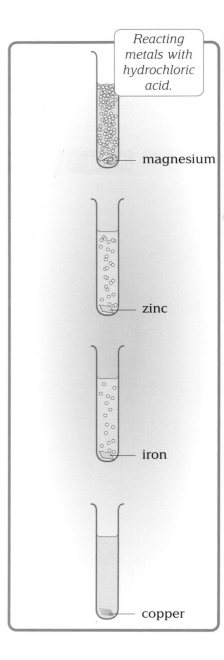

Reacting metals with hydrochloric acid.

magnesium

zinc

iron

copper

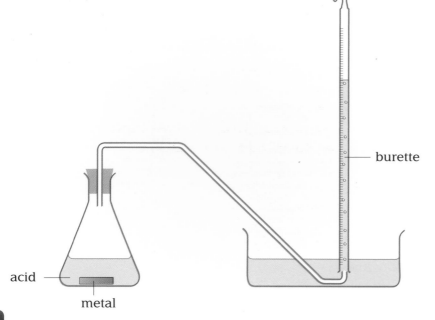

acid

metal

burette

The hydrogen produced pushes the water out of the burette.

Joy carried out this improved experiment and got the following results.

Time, in seconds	Volume of gas produced, in cm³			
	with copper	with magnesium	with iron	with zinc
30	0	4.0	1.0	1.5
60	0	8.0	3.0	3.0
90	0	13.0	5.0	6.0
120	0	18.0	7.0	9.0
150	0	22.5	9.0	12.0
180	0	26.0	10.5	14.0
210	0	28.0	11.5	15.5

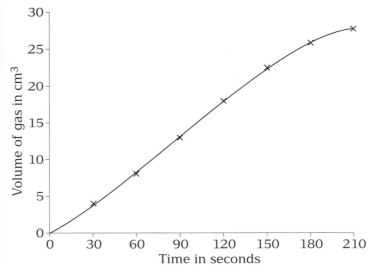

This graph shows the volume of hydrogen produced in the reaction with magnesium.

5 Look at the graph of the volume of hydrogen produced in the reaction with magnesium.

    a Plot a similar graph for iron and zinc.

    b Use these graphs to place the metals in order of reactivity.

6 Joy thinks that magnesium is twice as reactive as zinc.

    a What is her evidence?

    b Do you agree with her conclusion? Explain your answer.

Joy then decides that she will use this method to compare these four metals with another metal – aluminium.

These are Joy's results for aluminium.

7 Based on its position in the reactivity series, what results would <u>you</u> expect for aluminium?

8 Do these results match your prediction? Explain your answer.

Time in seconds	Volume in cm³
30	0.5
60	1.0
90	1.5
120	2.0
150	4.0
180	7.0
210	10.0

You should now understand the key words
and key ideas shown below.

- Metals will gradually react with the air and water from the atmosphere.
- Copper and gold will not **tarnish** even after a long time.
- Sodium and potassium tarnish so quickly that they need to be stored in oil.
- Sodium and potassium are **alkali metals**. They are soft and easy to cut.

- Some metals react with cold water to produce hydrogen.
- Some metals react more readily with water than others.

- Metals react with acids to produce hydrogen and a **salt**.
- Some metals react more readily with acids than others.
- Some metals do not react with acids.

- Metals react with oxygen to form oxides.
- The **reactivity series** for metals with oxygen is generally similar to that for water and acids.

- In a **displacement reaction,** a metal **displaces** a less reactive metal from a solution of one of its salts.
- We can use the order of **reactivity** of metals to make **predictions** about other metals that have not been observed.

- Metals have a variety of different uses.

- The reactivity of a metal affects its uses and the extraction method from its **ore**:
  - Less reactive metals such as iron are extracted by reacting the ore with carbon. The way iron is extracted from **haematite**.
  - Reactive metals such as sodium need to be extracted by **electrolysis**.

Environmental chemistry

In this unit we shall be studying some of the ways in which humans have polluted the world. We shall consider the evidence for acid rain and for global warming.

KEY WORDS
vegetation cover
acid rain
corrosion
catalytic converter
reliable
insufficient data
monitoring
air quality
indicator organisms
biased
global warming
greenhouse effect
climate change

9G.1 Are soils different from each other?

Soil is not the same all over the world. There are clay soils, sandy soils and chalky soils; there are dry soils and sticky soils. Local rocks, plants and soil animals all affect what the soil is like.

Weathering and erosion of rocks produce smaller pieces that become part of the soil. Dead plant and animal matter add humus to soil. As the humus breaks down further, it adds mineral nutrients to the soil. The amount of plant growth – also called **vegetation cover** – is therefore very important in the formation of soil. Soil animals make burrows that help air get into the soil. Plant roots need oxygen from the air.

These soil crumbs contain tiny bits of broken rock and animal and plant matter.

Gardeners dig compost and manure into soil. Compost is rotted plant material.

Earthworms make burrows that help air get into the soil.

1   Look at the photographs. How do earthworms and compost affect soil?

Some soils are good for lots of types of plants, some are good for a only a few types of plants, and others are no good for plants at all. One important factor in this is the acidity of the soil. Most plants grow best in soil that has a pH of between 6 and 8.

2 Find out what:

   a the pH scale measures;

   b pH 6 means;

   c pH 7 means;

   d pH 8 means.

Some plants grow well in soil that is acidic, other plants grow well in soil that is alkaline. The table gives some examples.

Plants for acidic soils	Plants for alkaline soils
crocus	cowslip
rhododendron	lilac
camellia	flowering cherry
chinese witch hazel	wallflower
good-luck plant	iris

3 Look at the photographs. Which garden has soil that is alkaline and which garden has soil that is acidic? Explain your answers.

4 What would you say to a gardener who wanted to grow rhododendrons and cowslips side-by-side?

Neutralising acid soils

Lots of farms and gardens have soils that are too acidic for many plants. We make these soils less acidic by adding powdered limestone or other forms of lime to neutralise some of the acid. Limestone is a naturally occurring form of calcium carbonate. It is cheap and plentiful in the UK.

Cowslips and a rhododendron bush growing in two different gardens.

5 Find out how farmers or gardeners test soil to see what its pH is.

6 What do scientists mean by <u>neutralise</u>?

9G.2 Acid rain

Acid rain falling on us sounds <u>really</u> nasty! It suggests that the rain will burn holes in our coats, burn away our skin and kill all the grass. We need to know some more about acid rain before we make up our minds.

A scientist goes to Ascension Island, which is in the middle of the Atlantic Ocean. It is a long way away from any pollution so the rain should be pure and clean. When the scientist collects some rainwater and tests it with universal indicator, the indicator turns yellow! This means its pH is about 5.5 – the rain is a weak acid. The conclusion is that <u>unpolluted</u> rain is acidic. Acidic rain is natural.

1   What does the test result tell us about the rain on Ascension Island?

2   What does <u>unpolluted</u> mean?

The scientist leaves Ascension Island and tests rainwater from Faxton, a town in a busy industrial part of England. This time the universal indicator turns orange. The pH of the rain is about 4. Something has made the rain more acidic than the rain on Ascension Island. The rain from Faxton has been <u>polluted</u>. This is what we mean by acid rain – rainwater with an <u>unusually</u> low pH due to pollution.

3   What does the test result tell us about the rain in Faxton?

4   What does <u>polluted</u> mean?

5   How is the rain in Faxton different from the rain in Ascension Island? Suggest a reason for the difference.

What does acid rain do to rocks and building materials?

The table shows what happens to some different kinds of rock when you add them to dilute acid.

Example of rock	What happens to the rock in acid
granite	little or no change
sandstone with a silica cement	little or no change
sandstone with a carbonate cement	falls apart as the cement reacts with the acid
limestone	fizzes and disappears
chalk	fizzes and disappears

6   What does acid do to chalk and limestone?

7   What does acid do to sandstone with a carbonate cement?

8   Explain what happens to sandstone with a carbonate cement in acid.

9   The rocks in the table are all building materials. Which <u>two</u> rocks would be best to use in Faxton? Explain your answer.

10 The statue has been eaten away by acid rain. What type of rock could it be made from?

Does anything else affect rocks in this way?

When something gets worn away we say that it is <u>weathered</u>. We see this happening to the rocks out in the countryside and to the building materials our homes are made of. It is not only acid rain that weathers rocks.

- <u>Plant roots</u> break tiny bits off rocks as they force their way into tiny cracks. The cracks get bigger and the rock breaks.

- <u>Rivers</u> gradually wear away the rocks on their riverbeds.

- In the winter, <u>water</u> in cracks in rocks freezes and expands. The rocks crack and bits break off when the ice melts.

- <u>Our feet</u> wear away rocks and paths as we walk over them.

All these changes are very slow, but they do happen.

11 How did the Grand Canyon form?

12 What wore away the steps?

13 What broke up the paving slabs?

Acid rain affects some metals

Acids also eat away some metals. This is called **corrosion**.

Acid rain is <u>very</u> dilute, but it has still corroded these metal railings faster than normal rain.

LEAD   IRON   ZINC

You can see the bubbles of hydrogen produced as metals react with acid. Notice that the lead is not reacting.

14 Which metal corrodes the fastest?

15 Which metal would you use to make a tank for holding acid? Explain your answer.

16 Why does it take a long time for metal railings to rust away?

What does acid rain do to plants?

Trees and other plants can survive the slight amount of acid that is naturally in rain, but the extra acidity caused by pollution can slowly kill them. The more acidic the rain, the faster minerals drain out of the soil. Some plants cannot survive the extra acidity and the shortage of minerals.

17 Look at the picture of the tree. In what ways does it look unhealthy?

What does acid rain do to animals?

Polluted rain has a pH of around 4. Humans can happily drink orange juice and cola, both of which are more acidic than this. Acid rain doesn't have much effect on large animals like us.

18 Which is more acidic, polluted rain or cola?

This tree's needles are falling off and it is dying! This is because it is growing in an area where the rain is very acidic.

Frogs, fish and other types of water life have a much bigger problem, however. All the rain drains into the lakes and rivers where they live. They can't get away from the acid.

- The acid stops the water creatures' eggs from hatching and it kills the young fish and tadpoles soon after they have hatched.

- Acid kills the water plants and insects that the older fish eat, and then the fish starve.

- Acidic water draining off the land carries extra aluminium, which stops a fish's gills working properly.

This gradual reduction in the number and variety of living things is called progressive depletion. The smaller and more acid-sensitive creatures disappear first. But, in the end, all the living things disappear.

There is nothing alive in this river.

19 Why does nothing live in the river?
Suggest at least <u>two</u> possible reasons.

9G.3 What causes acid rain?

The photographs all show things that help to cause acid rain. They are all putting one or more gases that can make acidic solutions into the air! Yes, Paul Scholes is doing this, not just when he plays football, but every time he breathes out. These gases mix in with the rest of the atmosphere, near the ground and high in the air. As rain falls through the air some of the gases dissolve. This makes the rain more acidic.

1 Name <u>four</u> things that put gases that make acidic rain into the air.

2 How do these four things give out these gases?

3 How do the gases make the rain acidic?

4 Why is the rain acidic even if you live far away from any industrial pollution?

All living things give out carbon dioxide. Volcanoes give out carbon dioxide and sulphur dioxide. Sulphur dioxide dissolves in rain to make a strong acid.

Cars, lorries and aircraft give out carbon dioxide, sulphur dioxide and nitrogen oxides. Nitrogen oxides dissolve in rain to make a strong acid. Power station chimneys give out carbon dioxide and sulphur dioxide. The atmosphere contains over 3 billion tonnes of carbon dioxide. It dissolves in water to form a very weak acid.

5 Identify all the sources of gases that make acid rain in the picture.

6 Which sources of these gases are natural and which are artificial?

7 Which of these gases does each source give out?

8 Which of these gases dissolve to form strong acids?

9 Trees are a source of carbon dioxide because they give out carbon dioxide at night. However, they use carbon dioxide during the day. In a typical 24-hour period, do trees make more carbon dioxide than they use, or not? Explain your answer.

9G.4 Can we reduce the amount of acid in the rain?

Human beings can be lazy and greedy! Our cars and industries release a lot of gases that can dissolve to form acid rain into the air, and we have done little to stop this, or even to reduce it. We could:

- use more renewable energy sources;
- burn less fuel;
- remove the sulphur from fossil fuels before we burn them;
- remove the gases from chimney smoke and car exhaust fumes.

All these things take effort and cost money. But we must do it – there is only one Earth; when we pollute it, we still have to live on it.

1 Why have people done so little about reducing pollution?

2 Why is it important to reduce pollution?

Making car exhausts cleaner

The gases that come out of the exhaust pipe of a car are called its emissions. These emissions include nitrogen oxides, sulphur dioxide and carbon monoxide. Carbon monoxide is the gas that makes car exhaust fumes so poisonous.

We can use **catalytic converters** to make the nitrogen oxide gases react with the carbon monoxide gas in the exhaust.

nitrogen oxides + carbon monoxide → nitrogen + carbon dioxide

Inside the catalytic converter the substance that does this job is called the catalyst. The catalyst slowly gets dirty and this stops it from working, so occasionally it has to be replaced. A replacement costs around £300, so it is not cheap.

The catalytic converter is in the car's exhaust system. Catalysts on special surfaces inside the converter speed up the reactions that make the exhaust gases less polluting.

3 Why are nitrogen oxides bad for the environment?

4 Why is carbon monoxide dangerous?

5 Where is a catalytic converter fitted on a car?

6 What does a catalytic converter do?

7 Why do catalytic converters need to be replaced sometimes?

8 Why might a car owner not be pleased about having to replace the catalytic converter?

9 By law, all new cars in the UK must have a catalytic converter. Make a guess of how many cars there are in the street where you live. Now work out the cost of fitting a catalytic converter to all of them.

Catalytic converters cannot reduce the amount of sulphur dioxide in the exhaust emissions. That is why low sulphur petrol was developed. There is still some sulphur in the petrol though, and this causes the familiar 'eggy' smell from the exhaust when a car hasn't quite warmed up.

 10 How does using low sulphur petrol help to prevent acid rain?

The gases that come out of the chimneys of a power station are also called emissions. These emissions include sulphur dioxide. It is possible to remove the sulphur dioxide, but it is expensive.

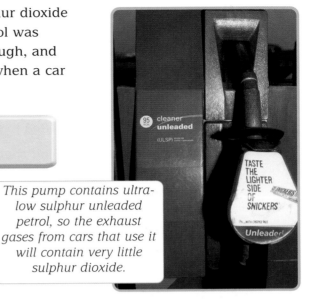

This pump contains ultra-low sulphur unleaded petrol, so the exhaust gases from cars that use it will contain very little sulphur dioxide.

Air quality

Scientists need to know whether or not air pollution is getting worse. First, they must collect information. This information is called <u>data</u>. It must be collected accurately and carefully, so that it can be relied on. Enough data must be collected for the scientists to be sure that it reflects general trends. Otherwise, the data could be just the records of a few days of unusual air pollution. Data that is collected accurately, carefully and in a sufficient amount is said to be **reliable**. If the scientists don't have enough data for making a good decision, they say they have **insufficient data**.

Scientists measure the amounts of pollutants in the air every day. We call this **monitoring** the **air quality**. To 'monitor' something means to measure it regularly, so that any changes will be detected.

 11 What is the difference between <u>testing</u> air quality and <u>monitoring</u> it?

12 Which air pollutants do local authorities monitor?

 13 Why do local authorities put air quality tables in local newspapers?

	low	moderate	high	very high
index	(1-3)	(4-6)	(7-9)	(10)
sulphur dioxide (ppb)	less than 100	100–199	200–399	400+
ozone (ppb)	less than 50	50–89	80–179	180+
carbon monoxide (ppm)	less than 10	10–14	15–19	20+
nitrogen dioxide (ppb)	less than 150	150–299	300–399	400+
particles(PM_{10}) (mcg per m^{-3})	less than 50	50–74	75–99	100+

UK Department of the Environment standard for air quality

	London	Leeds	Hull
sulphur dioxide (ppb)	50	44	57
ozone (ppb)	14	15	30
carbon monoxide (ppm)	11	9	6
nitrogen dioxide (ppb)	38	16	8
particles(PM_{10}) (mcg per m^{-3})	22	16	24

Data for April 1

Air quality tables are published in newspapers. Sometimes people with breathing problems are warned to stay indoors as much as possible.

One way to monitor air quality is to use pumps to suck air through special tubes called <u>sorbent tubes</u>. These tubes contain filters and chemicals. The chemicals in the tubes trap pollutant gases, such as the gases that cause acid rain. The filters trap the smoke and soot particles that come from vehicle exhausts and chimneys. These particles can irritate our lungs and throats, and cause bronchitis and asthma to get worse.

By analysing the filters and chemicals in the tubes every day, scientists know how much of each pollutant there is. Rain is monitored too. Scientists put rain gauges (also called rain collectors) in open spaces all over the world. Each rain gauge is checked every day. Scientists can tell from the amount of water in the gauge how much rain has fallen during the day. By analysing the water they can find out how acidic the rain is and whether or not it contains other pollutants too.

We can also learn about air quality in a particular area by monitoring the plant life. Some plant species can only grow in clean air. We call these species **indicator organisms**.

glass wool filter for trapping smoke and soot particles

layers of chemicals to trap pollutant gases from the air

This sort of tube is called a sorbent tube. It is used for monitoring air quality.

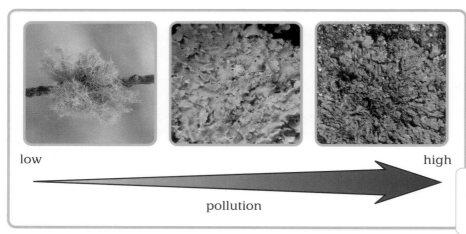

low   high

pollution

The cleaner the air, the more species of lichens there are. Shrubby lichens grow only in air with very low concentrations of sulphur dioxide.

14 Do you think that the number of species of lichens would <u>increase</u> or <u>decrease</u> as you go out from a city centre? Give reasons for your answer.

15 In a churchyard near a power station, there are no lichens growing on the gravestones. The leaves on a sycamore tree have no tar spots on them.

   a What does this suggest about the air quality in the churchyard?

   b What could be affecting the air quality?

   c Do you think the churchyard gives the scientist sufficient data to come to a definite conclusion?

The 'tar spots' on these sycamore leaves are caused by a fungus that grows only where the air is clean.

Through monitoring our air and rain quality, we can state, without guesswork, whether the air pollution is increasing, staying the same, or decreasing. We can decide whether or not our actions to reduce pollution are working.

It would not be right to leave all the monitoring to the people who run power stations and factories and to the car makers. It is possible that they might be biased. To be **biased** means to present facts or draw conclusions in a way that suits you or your organisation, rather than telling the strict truth.

 16 Car manufacturers might be biased in reporting how clean their cars' exhausts are. Suggest reasons for this.

Photographic and historical evidence

We can also learn about the changing nature of air and rain quality from old photographs and books, or even just by looking around.

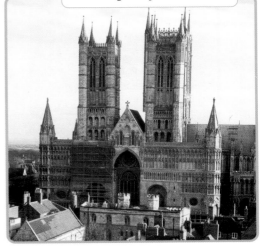

In 2000 there was a lot of scaffolding on Lincoln Cathedral whilst repairs were made to stonework damaged by acid rain.

This photograph of Lincoln Cathedral taken in 1900 shows a building that has suffered very little damage from air pollution in six hundred years. The statues and carved stones still looked detailed and beautiful.

Written records can also teach us much. Life in Widnes in Victorian times must have been grim. Historical accounts say there was not one green leaf or blade of grass in the town. We believe that this was due to emissions from the local chemical industry, which caused the rain there to be <u>pH 1</u>. Nowadays, Widnes is a normal town, with gardens and parks.

These chemical workers in Widnes wore goggles and had every scrap of skin covered to protect them from the acidic gases produced by the industry they worked in.

 17 Explain how the photographs and their captions provide evidence that pollution has got better in one place but has got worse in another place.

9G.5 Is global warming really happening?

The data collected on air temperatures, wind and rainfall has enabled scientists to come to a startling conclusion. This conclusion is that the average temperature of the Earth is higher now than it was 100 years ago. The increase in temperature of just over 0.5 °C doesn't sound much. However, most of this increase has happened in the last 20 years. Some scientists fear that the average surface temperature of the Earth could rise by up to 5 °C by the year 2100. They call it **global warming** and it would be serious.

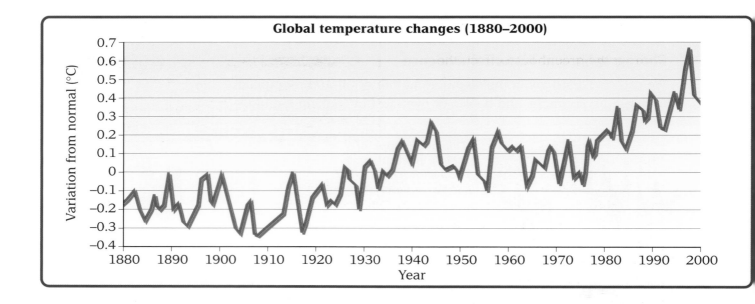

Global temperature changes (1880–2000)

1 By how much could the average surface temperature of the Earth rise by the year 2100?

2 Look at the graph.

  a What general trend does the graph show?

  b Find a 50-year period during which the temperature trend hardly changed.

  c Find a 30-year period during which the temperature trend went down slightly.

  d Find the 20-year period during which the temperature trend went up the most.

The greenhouse effect

The Sun's rays continually heat the Earth. Fortunately, the Earth doesn't just get hotter and hotter because it also radiates heat back into space. Some gases in the atmosphere reduce this heat loss. The gases trap heat like a duvet on a bed or the glass in a greenhouse, with the result that the average temperature of the Earth stays more or less the same. This is called the **greenhouse effect**. The greenhouse effect is a <u>natural</u> effect, not a consequence of air pollution. Without the greenhouse effect, the Earth would be a much colder planet.

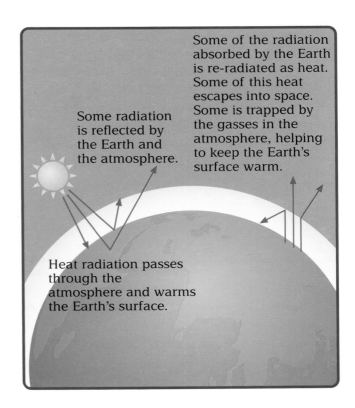

Some radiation is reflected by the Earth and the atmosphere.

Some of the radiation absorbed by the Earth is re-radiated as heat. Some of this heat escapes into space. Some is trapped by the gasses in the atmosphere, helping to keep the Earth's surface warm.

Heat radiation passes through the atmosphere and warms the Earth's surface.

Global warming

One of the main gases responsible for the greenhouse effect is carbon dioxide. The more carbon dioxide there is in the air, the warmer the Earth will be. Before human industry began to pollute the air, the Earth's atmosphere had been in a finely balanced position for millions of years. Photosynthesis by plants used up carbon dioxide, and respiration by plants and animals made carbon dioxide. The amount of carbon dioxide stayed constant at around 0.03% of the air. This was just enough to cause a greenhouse effect that kept the Earth at a suitable temperature for the life on the planet. It was like a perfect duvet, one you would never want to change.

3 Is the greenhouse effect natural or caused by humans?

4 a Name <u>one</u> gas responsible for the greenhouse effect.

   b State <u>one</u> natural process that uses up this gas and <u>one</u> natural process that makes this gas.

If you put a thicker duvet on your bed tonight you would be warmer – possibly even too hot. In a similar way, as we increase the amount of carbon dioxide in the atmosphere, the Earth gets warmer. Nearly all scientists believe that global warming is happening and that the extra carbon dioxide is the cause.

Our lives at home and the successful working of the industries that make our goods and possessions rely on electricity. Worldwide, most electricity is generated in power stations that burn fossil fuels – coal, oil and gas. Our road transport uses petrol or diesel, and jet aircraft burn kerosene. All of these fossil fuels contain carbon, so when they burn they release carbon dioxide. Our increasing use of fossil fuels for making electricity and for transport explains why carbon dioxide levels are rising.

Might climate change mean this?

 5 Explain <u>two</u> ways that human activity increases the amount of carbon dioxide in the air.

As the world warms up, weather patterns everywhere will change. This is called **climate change**. Not everyone agrees about exactly how weather patterns will change. For parts of the world this will be pleasant. Some people think that the climate in the UK might become more like that of Spain. Elsewhere the changes will not be welcome. Great deserts, such as the Sahara, could increase in size and eventually cover much land that is fertile today. As the oceans warm up they will expand. This effect, along with water released by melting ice caps, will cause sea levels to rise, flooding low-lying land around the world. The worst predictions are that over 75% of land in England would flood permanently. Wales, Scotland and Ireland would keep a higher percentage of dry land, as they are more hilly.

or this?

 6 What effect of global warming does each cartoon illustrate?

The scientists of the world do not all agree on whether or not increased amounts of carbon dioxide are causing global warming. They <u>do</u> agree that global warming <u>is</u> happening, but some claim that it is part of a natural cycle of an ice age followed by a warming up period, then another ice age, and so on. These scientists believe we are in the warming up period following the ice age that ended 11 000 years ago. However, 9 out of 10 weather scientists believe that global warming is caused by increased amounts of carbon dioxide.

or this?

 7 What are the <u>two</u> possible causes of global warming?
8 What percentage of weather scientists believe in each of the possible causes?

You should now understand the key words and key ideas shown below.

Key words
vegetation cover
acid rain
corrosion
catalytic converter
reliable
insufficient data
monitoring
air quality
indicator organisms
biased
global warming
greenhouse effect
climate change

KEY IDEAS

- Rocks and building materials are slowly weathered and eroded.

- Soil forms from the interactions between rock fragments and living things.

- Different soils can have different pH values, making them suitable for different plants.

- Acidic soils can be made less acidic by adding lime.

- Rain is naturally slightly acidic due to dissolved carbon dioxide.

- Nitrogen oxides and sulphur dioxide gases are produced by human industrial activity. They increase the acidity of rain.

- As rain becomes more acidic, the weathering and erosion of rocks and building materials speeds up.

- Acid rain corrodes some metals, and is damaging to some life forms.

- The use of low sulphur petrol and catalytic converters in cars can reduce the emissions that cause acid rain.

- Air and water quality are closely monitored and measured.

- The Earth's atmosphere reduces heat loss into space. This is the greenhouse effect.

- The Earth's climate is getting warmer. We call this global warming.

- Global warming is probably due to increased amounts of carbon dioxide in the atmosphere.

Using chemistry

In this unit we shall be finding out more about using chemicals as an energy source and seeing how to make new materials. We shall use word equations and symbol equations to represent chemical reactions. We shall also discover how atoms are rearranged, but not lost or made, during a chemical reaction.

9H.1 What chemical reactions take place when fuels burn?

In Units 7F and 9F you saw how burning chemicals is called combustion. Combustion does not always involve flames, smoke and sparks. It involves a rapid reaction with oxygen from the air to make new substances, called oxides. Oxides are compounds that contain oxygen and one other element.

1   Name three oxides you have seen in earlier science work.

Combustion and oxides

When we burn a substance, the oxygen from the air reacts with elements and compounds in the substance to form oxides. Sometimes this is difficult to see because the reactions involve colourless gases such as oxygen and carbon dioxide.

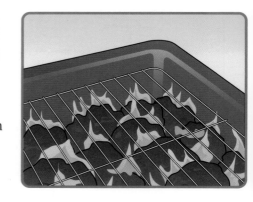

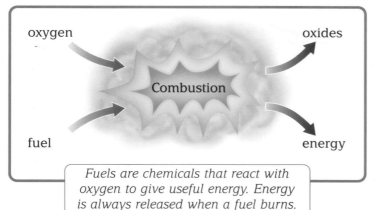

oxygen + fuel → Combustion → oxides + energy

Fuels are chemicals that react with oxygen to give useful energy. Energy is always released when a fuel burns.

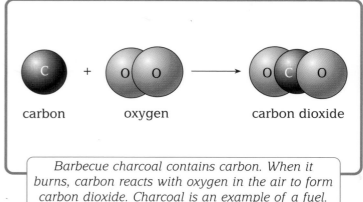

carbon + oxygen → carbon dioxide

Barbecue charcoal contains carbon. When it burns, carbon reacts with oxygen in the air to form carbon dioxide. Charcoal is an example of a fuel.

2 Name the substances formed when:

a iron burns;

b hydrogen undergoes combustion.

3 Write down a process in the human body that is similar to combustion.

The gas that is used in gas cookers and in Bunsen burners is called natural gas. Its chemical name is methane. It belongs to a group of compounds called **hydrocarbons**. Hydrocarbons contain hydrogen and carbon only.

We get natural gas from rocks below the surface of the North Sea.

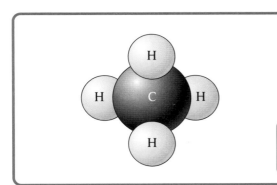

A molecule of methane contains one carbon atom and four hydrogen atoms. It has the formula CH_4.

4 What type of compound is methane?

5 How many atoms does a methane molecule contain?

We can write an equation for the combustion of methane:

methane + oxygen → carbon dioxide + hydrogen oxide (water) + energy

$$CH_4 + 2O_2 \rightarrow CO_2 + 2H_2O + energy$$

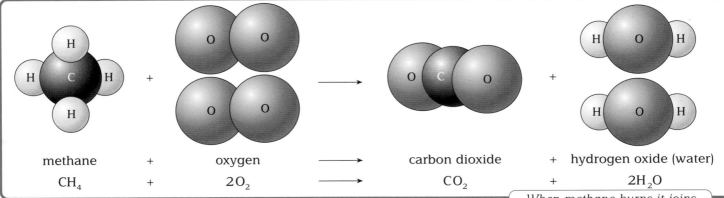

methane + oxygen ⟶ carbon dioxide + hydrogen oxide (water)

$$CH_4 + 2O_2 \longrightarrow CO_2 + 2H_2O$$

When methane burns it joins up with oxygen in the air to form the oxides carbon dioxide and water.

6 How many molecules of water are made when one molecule of methane is burnt completely?

Not completely burnt

Sometimes there is not enough air for fuels to burn completely.
We call this **incomplete combustion**.

7 Why does incomplete combustion happen?

Look at the diagrams to see the different products of complete
and incomplete combustion of methane.

*Water and carbon
dioxide are formed
when the air hole is open.*

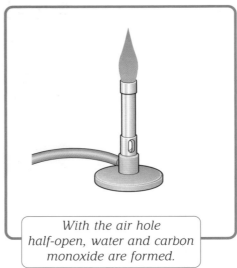

*With the air hole
half-open, water and carbon
monoxide are formed.*

*With the air hole closed,
water and carbon are formed.*

This is the reaction when the air hole is half-open:

methane + oxygen → carbon monoxide + hydrogen oxide + energy

$$2CH_4 + 3O_2 \rightarrow 2CO + 4H_2O + energy$$

When the air hole is closed even less oxygen is available from
the air:

methane + oxygen → carbon + hydrogen oxide + energy

$$CH_4 + O_2 \rightarrow C + 2H_2O + energy$$

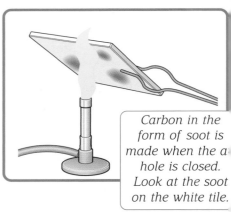

*Carbon in the
form of soot is
made when the a
hole is closed.
Look at the soot
on the white tile.*

8 As you slowly close the air hole of a Bunsen
burner what gas is cut off from the flame?

9 Which gas provides the carbon that appears
as soot in the flame?

10 Describe how a 'safe' Bunsen burner flame in
a school laboratory uses incomplete combustion
to show that the Bunsen burner is lit.

*The small dust-like
particles of soot
become very hot in
the flame. They glow
like thousands of
miniature lamps,
making the flame
yellow and luminous.
This is how candles,
oil lamps and
lanterns make light
by burning a fuel.*

Incomplete combustion can be dangerous

Gas fires and gas central heating boilers use methane as fuel. If there is plenty of air, carbon dioxide and water are formed. They escape out of a type of chimney called a flue.

Incomplete combustion happens when too little air reaches the flame. The flame contains carbon monoxide gas and is yellow with glowing carbon. Carbon monoxide is poisonous and has no smell.

You can sometimes see the water produced in combustion as steam.

Two students die – faulty gas fire blamed

 11 How can you tell if a gas fire is not working properly?

 12 Find out why you should not put damp washing on top of gas fires and central heating boilers, even if you think there is very little chance of the washing catching fire.

Incomplete combustion causes pollution

Vehicle fuels are hydrocarbons and are never completely burnt. Carbon dioxide, carbon monoxide, oxides of nitrogen made from burnt nitrogen, water and sometimes soot are formed. Most of these substances are harmful pollutants in our air.

 13 Find out how the oxides of nitrogen are made by combustion in a hot car engine.

You can see the water as steam from a car's exhaust on a cold day. You cannot see the colourless pollutant carbon monoxide.

Matches, fireworks and explosives

Chemicals can be used in spectacular ways in very rapid combustion reactions. These uses of chemistry are called <u>pyrotechnics</u>.

Special chemicals containing their own oxygen are used in pyrotechnics.

Some chemicals contain the oxygen needed for combustion in their molecules. Examples are potassium nitrate (KNO_3), potassium chlorate ($KClO_3$) and potassium permanganate ($KMnO_4$). These compounds contain a lot of oxygen atoms.

14 How many oxygen atoms are there in one molecule of:

  a potassium nitrate;

  b potassium chlorate;

  c potassium permanganate?

Compounds containing two elements and oxygen have names ending in '-ate'. Some of these compounds are called <u>oxidising agents</u>, because they are good at giving up oxygen to other chemicals. Adding oxygen like this is called **oxidation**.
The oxygen in the oxidising agents can rapidly react with other chemicals to cause explosions, even under water.

15 How are the three potassium compounds named to show that they contain oxygen?

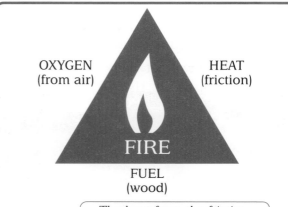

Combustion using the oxygen in an oxidising agent makes a fast reaction called an explosion.

How matches work

Match heads contain a mixture of chemicals. They use the reaction between sulphur and phosphorus and an oxidising agent called potassium chlorate.

16 Write down the formula for potassium chlorate and the symbols for sulphur and phosphorus.

Friction when you strike a match makes the oxidising agent release oxygen. The sulphur and phosphorus burn in the oxygen, giving out a lot of heat.

OXYGEN (from air)   HEAT (friction)

FIRE

FUEL (wood)

The heat from the friction, the wood in the match and oxygen in the air make a fire triangle, so the match burns.

17 What is the fuel in the burning match, as shown in the fire triangle?

18 What group of chemicals provides the heat in the triangle?

9H.2 Chemical reactions as energy resources

Chemicals make other useful forms of energy besides heat. For example, we use chemicals in **cells** and batteries to make electricity.

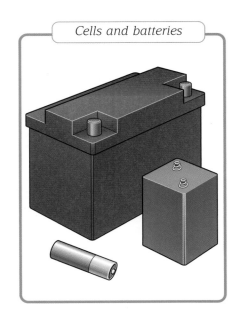

 1 Why do we often use cells, instead of a mains supply, as a source of electricity?

There are many types of cells. The different types have special names such as nickel–cadmium, lead–acid or lithium cells. Many cells contain elements such as zinc, copper, lead, manganese, mercury or silver. These elements are metals. Metals are nearly always used in cells. Even gold has been used.

 2 What sort of element is most often used to make a cell?

You can use a pair of different metals dipped into dilute sulphuric acid to make a cell. The pieces of metal that dip into the acid are called <u>electrodes</u>.

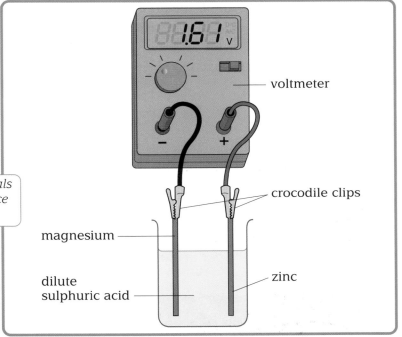

Different pairs of metals dipped in acid produce different voltages.

voltmeter

crocodile clips

magnesium

dilute sulphuric acid

zinc

The voltage produced depends on the difference in reactivity between the two metals.

Negative electrode	Positive electrode	Approximate reading on the voltmeter
magnesium	copper	2.71V
magnesium	iron	1.93V
magnesium	zinc	1.61V

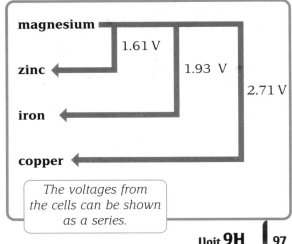

magnesium
1.61 V
zinc
1.93 V
iron
2.71 V
copper

The voltages from the cells can be shown as a series.

 3 Which pair of metals would make the best cell?

4 Work out how many volts you get from a cell that uses zinc and copper electrodes.

Scientists put metals in very special and carefully controlled cells and measured the voltages produced. Look at their results.

K	3.26 V	Zn	1.11 V
Na	3.05 V	Fe	0.78 V
Mg	2.71 V	Pb	0.47 V
Al	2.00 V	Cu	0.00 V

This series is called the **electrochemical series**.

 5 Which metal is the highest in the series and which metal is the lowest?

Reactivity of metals

In Unit 9F you saw how to construct and use a reactivity series of metals. You also saw how to compare pairs of metals by using <u>displacement reactions</u>. Displacement reactions happen when a reactive metal is placed in a solution of a salt of a less reactive metal. For example:

zinc + copper sulphate → zinc sulphate + copper
$$Zn + CuSO_4 \rightarrow ZnSO_4 + Cu$$

 6 Is zinc higher up or lower down the electrochemical series than copper?

 7 Do you think magnesium will displace copper from copper sulphate solution? Explain your answer.

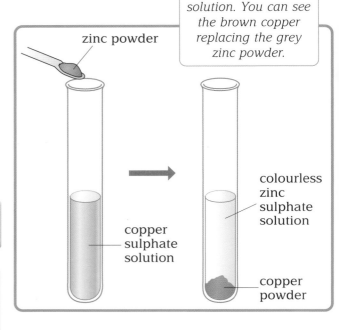

zinc powder

The reactive zinc displaces the less reactive copper from copper sulphate solution. You can see the brown copper replacing the grey zinc powder.

colourless zinc sulphate solution

copper sulphate solution

copper powder

Copper, silver and gold are unreactive metals, so people have used them to make coins for thousands of years.

Silver is an unreactive metal and is even more unreactive than copper. Experiments with cells show that copper gives a voltage when paired with silver. Silver is so unreactive that it gives a negative reading on the voltmeter.

Cu	0.00 V	Ag	–0.46 V

Copper should displace silver from a solution of a silver salt.

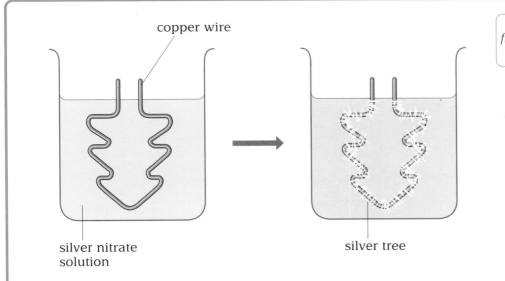

copper wire

silver nitrate
solution

silver tree

The copper displaces the silver from the silver nitrate solution to make a 'silver tree'.

The equation for the displacement of silver by copper is:

copper + silver nitrate → silver + copper nitrate

$$Cu + 2AgNO_3 \rightarrow 2Ag + Cu(NO_3)_2$$

8 Predict another reaction between a metal and silver nitrate that might be a displacement reaction.

Heat and reactions

There are many chemical reactions that produce temperature changes but do not involve combustion. For example, heat is released when concentrated sulphuric acid is diluted and when plaster of Paris sets.

Hand warmers use heat from a chemical reaction that does not use combustion.

9 Why do you think that sulphuric acid is <u>not</u> used in hand warmers?

9H.3 What new materials can chemical reactions make?

Chemists keep finding new ways to make useful molecules from basic resources such as minerals and plants.

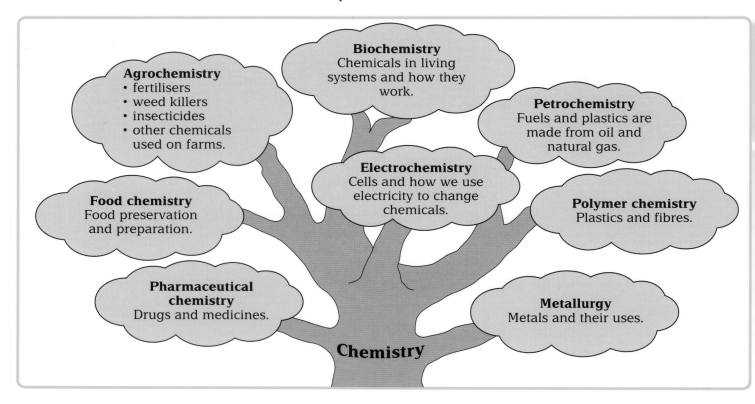

Agrochemistry
• fertilisers
• weed killers
• insecticides
• other chemicals used on farms.

Biochemistry
Chemicals in living systems and how they work.

Petrochemistry
Fuels and plastics are made from oil and natural gas.

Food chemistry
Food preservation and preparation.

Electrochemistry
Cells and how we use electricity to change chemicals.

Polymer chemistry
Plastics and fibres.

Pharmaceutical chemistry
Drugs and medicines.

Metallurgy
Metals and their uses.

Chemistry

1   Name <u>four</u> chemicals produced or used by your body.

2   List <u>three</u> fuels made by the petrochemical industry.

3   List <u>three</u> different artificial fabrics.

4   Find out which metals are used to make modern coins. Write your answer using chemical symbols.

5   Look at the different types of cells used in your house. Draw a diagram of <u>two</u> types and write down their cell voltage.

6   Look at the labels on food jars, tins and packages, and list the chemicals in <u>three</u> of them.

Living materials contain very large and complicated molecules, such as proteins and DNA.

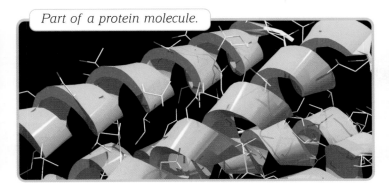
Part of a protein molecule.

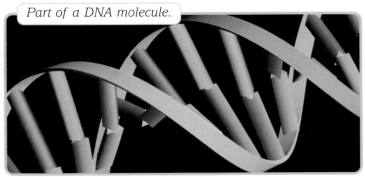
Part of a DNA molecule.

The human body contains millions of different chemicals, made up from about 40 different elements.

7   Name <u>three</u> elements that are found in the human body.

Plants also contain lots of different chemicals. Our first painkillers came from plants.

How we got Aspirin

Hippocrates was a Greek philosopher who lived about 2500 years ago. He studied and practised medicine. He used a medicine made from the bark and leaves of willow trees to cure headaches and other pains.

Hippocrates is known as the father of medicine.

8   Write down <u>three</u> modern painkilling medicines.

In the 18th century, clergymen and doctors started to use willow as a painkiller again. They had discovered the idea in some ancient texts.

9   Do you think that all natural plant medicines are safe?

People thought that willow trees contained a secret ingredient that could cure pain.

Scientists tried to find out which of the chemicals in the willow tree was the painkiller. In the 1820s they finally extracted and identified the painkilling chemical.

Unfortunately, salicin caused side effects such as stomach aches, it made some people feel sick and they got bad indigestion.

In 1899 a chemical company reacted salicin with other chemicals to change it. The new drug was tested on some patients in a **trial**. A trial is where animals and then volunteer patients are tested with a new drug before it goes on sale. The side effects were few and the drug was renamed 'aspirin'.

Salix is the Latin name for a willow tree, so the chemical was named 'salicin'.

10 Aspirin can be used as a medicine for many illnesses. Find out about <u>one</u> illness where aspirin can be used.

Making new molecules is called <u>synthesis</u>. New chemicals that do not occur in nature are often made by synthesis. So they are called <u>synthetic</u> materials. Scientists join atoms and molecules together in different ways with bonds.

9H.4 Atoms and molecules in new materials

Making and breaking bonds is chemistry

When chemical reactions happen, the bonds in the starting molecules are broken and new bonds are made in the molecules that you end up with. Energy is released or taken in to make these changes.

The models of molecules show what happens when barbecue charcoal burns. Bonds are broken. Then new bonds are made to make carbon dioxide.

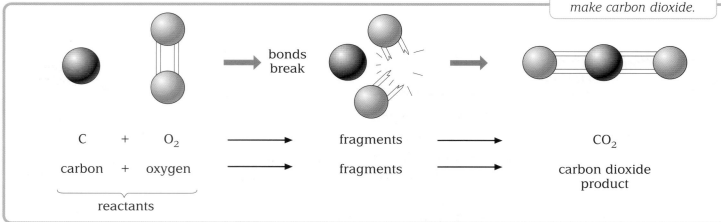

| C | + | O$_2$ | | fragments | | CO$_2$ |

carbon + oxygen → fragments → carbon dioxide product

reactants

1 Is energy released when charcoal burns?

The number of atoms is the same before and after the reaction. This means that the amount of material you have before the reaction starts and the amount you have when the reaction finishes are the same. No mass is lost. This rule is called the **law of conservation of mass**, and it works for all chemical reactions. In any reaction only the bonds are broken and made, not the atoms.

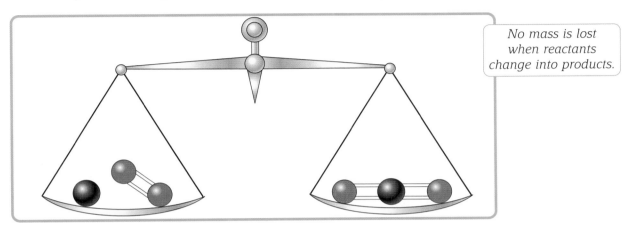

No mass is lost when reactants change into products.

When a candle burns, it looks like the law of conservation of mass is not being obeyed.

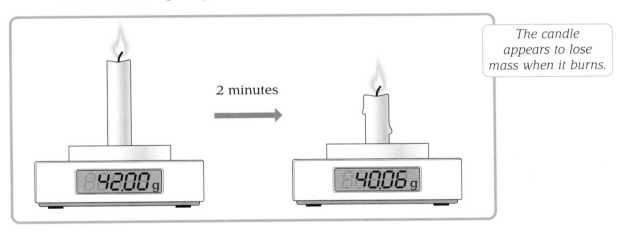

2 minutes

The candle appears to lose mass when it burns.

 2 How much mass has the candle lost while burning?

When the candle burns, it uses up oxygen from the air and produces water vapour and carbon dioxide. These gases escape into the air and so the candle seems to lose mass.

 3 Where does the lost mass of the candle go?

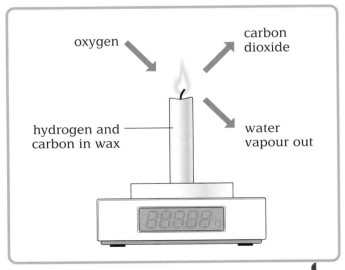

oxygen

carbon dioxide

hydrogen and carbon in wax

water vapour out

When all the oxygen, the escaping water vapour and the carbon dioxide are weighed, you can see that there is <u>no</u> change in mass. The law of conservation of mass <u>is</u> obeyed.

Burning a large mass of wood or a similar fuel seems to show a large loss of mass and leave just a little ash.

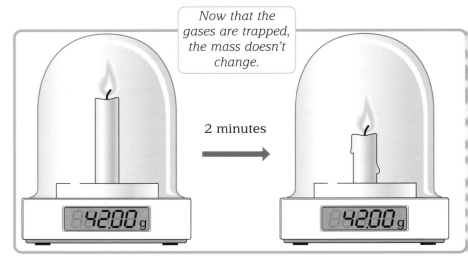

Now that the gases are trapped, the mass doesn't change.

2 minutes

4 Where does the mass of the burning wood go?

A theory about burning

In the late 1600s, two German chemists, called Johann Becher and Georg Stahl, made a new theory about burning. They thought metals, minerals and substances that could burn contained a substance called '**phlogiston**'. Phlogiston was given out during combustion in the form of fire, flames and light.

Scientists thought that:

- phlogiston was taken up by the air;

- there was a limit to the amount of phlogiston the air could take up;

- if you burned a candle in a closed vessel, the flame soon went out because the air inside had taken up all the phlogiston it could hold.

The air becomes saturated with phlogiston.

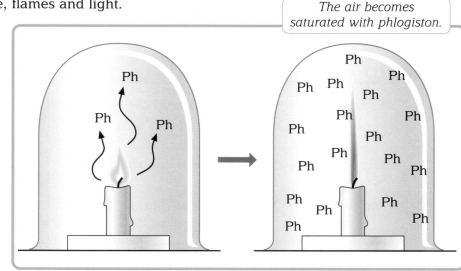

Normal air was called 'dephlogisticated' because it contained no phlogiston. When Joseph Priestley discovered <u>oxygen</u>, he believed it to be the purest 'dephlogisticated' air, which would rapidly take up phlogiston when things burned.

From about 1680 to 1800 most scientists accepted the phlogiston theory.

At first the French scientist Antoine Lavoisier believed in phlogiston. He carried out many experiments in which he weighed things before and after heating and burning. He used a balance that could weigh to 0.0005 g. He discovered that substances <u>gained</u> mass from the air when they burned.

Antoine Lavoisier lived during the time of the French Revolution. It was a time when many old ideas and theories were challenged.

5 If the phlogiston theory is true, what should happen to the mass when something burns?

From his experiments, Lavoisier discovered the law of conservation of mass as well as the role of oxygen in combustion. On the 5th September 1775, Lavoisier presented his ideas to the French Academy of Science. This is a translation of parts of the paper he published in 1777:

> I venture to propose to the Academy today a new theory of combustion. Materials may not burn except in a very few kinds of air, or rather, combustion may take place in only a single variety of air: that which … has been named dephlogisticated air and which I name here pure air. In all combustion, pure air in which the combustion takes place is destroyed or decomposed and the burning body increases in weight exactly in proportion to the quantity of air destroyed or decomposed.

This paper destroyed the theory of phlogiston. Soon no one believed in phlogiston. All scientists now agreed that oxygen was used in combustion.

6 Lavoisier showed that burning a substance in air decreases the mass of the air. What did the phlogiston theory say happens to the mass of the air during burning?

7 From our knowledge today, which gases do you think make up 'dephlogisticated' air?

You should now understand the key words and key ideas shown below.

There is never a loss or gain of mass in chemical reactions. This rule is called the **law of conservation of mass**.

The **electrochemical series** can be used to predict displacement reactions.

Cells made of pairs of metals in acid make different voltages and can be put in a list called the electrochemical series.

When new materials are made in a chemical reaction, the bonds in the molecules are broken and new bonds are made.

Cells and batteries use metals and other chemicals to make useful electricity.

Useful chemistry

Chemistry is used to make useful energy, to keep us well fed and healthy, and to make useful new materials.

Some chemical reactions give out heat energy without flames or combustion, and are used as hand warmers.

Trials are the tests that scientists carry out before a new product goes on sale.

North Sea gas is an important fuel and contains methane. Methane is a **hydrocarbon**, which means it contains hydrogen and carbon only.

Combustion involves adding oxygen from the air to chemicals to make energy and new substances called oxides.

Complete combustion happens when methane burns completely in air, to make carbon dioxide and hydrogen oxide (water).

Oxidation occurs when oxygen is added to other chemicals.

Incomplete combustion of methane happens when there is not enough oxygen available.

The '**phlogiston**' theory was popular for two centuries until oxygen and oxides were discovered. Theories about combustion had to change.

Energy and electricity

In this unit, we shall study different energy transfers, and in particular the way electricity is used to transfer energy to do useful things. We shall investigate voltage and energy transfers round a circuit. We will also study how electricity is generated, and how this can affect the environment.

KEY WORDS
transform
transfer
device
chemical energy
fossil fuels
potential energy
kinetic energy
thermal energy
appliances
components
ammeter
voltage
potential difference
voltmeter
pylon
substation
National Grid
generator
nuclear fuels
radiation energy

9I.1 How is energy involved in doing useful things?

In Unit 7I you learnt about different forms of energy. Whenever anything useful happens, one type of energy is changed (**transformed**) into another type of energy. A radio transforms electrical energy into sound energy, and **transfers** it to the surroundings.

Anything that changes energy from one form into another is called a **device**. We can group devices by the energy they use, for example devices that use electrical energy include toasters, DVD players and hairdryers even though they all give out different forms of energy. Other devices are grouped by the energy that they give out, for example heaters give out thermal energy. However, heaters use different forms of energy, for example electrical, or chemical energy, which is stored in coal, gas or oil.

1 How can devices be grouped?

2 Name <u>two</u> devices mentioned in the text.

3 Look at the photograph and write down <u>three</u> things that need electrical energy to work.

When we say that something 'uses electricity', we mean that electrical energy is changed into other useful forms of energy. Try to talk about electrical energy instead of electricity!

Some forms of energy can be stored for later use. Candles store **chemical energy** in their wax. During a power cut, a lit candle transforms this chemical energy into light and **thermal** (heat) **energy**. Chemical energy is also stored in **fossil fuels** such as oil, coal and gas, in food and in batteries.

Another way of storing energy is to give an object **potential energy** by changing its shape or by lifting it up. Springs in clockwork toys, a blown-up balloon or a stretched elastic band all store potential energy because their shape has been changed. This is called elastic potential energy. A skateboarder at the top of a ramp, and a person on a diving board have potential energy because of their positions. This is called gravitational potential energy.

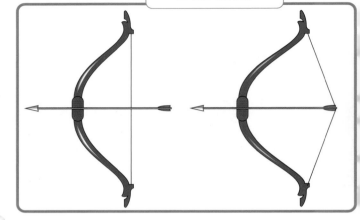

Stretching the bow stores elastic energy which is transferred to the arrow.

4 Write down <u>two</u> forms of energy that chemical energy can be turned into.

5 What has to change for an object to gain:

a elastic potential energy;

b gravitational energy?

6 Which of these examples have stored potential energy:

a water at the top of a waterslide;

b a child at the bottom of a slide;

c a peanut butter sandwich;

d an aeroplane in the sky;

e a stretched spring?

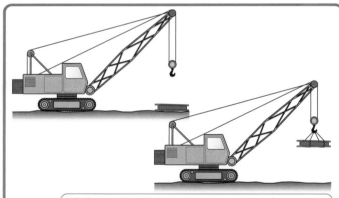

Lifting the girder gives it potential energy. If the girder falls, the gravitational potential energy is changed into kinetic energy.

Electrical energy cannot easily be stored but it is useful because it can be changed into so many other forms of energy. It is also a convenient and clean form of energy. Rechargeable batteries for mobile phones are charged up from the mains electricity supply, but the electrical energy changes into chemical energy before it is stored in the battery pack.

Chemical energy stored in the battery pack changes into electrical energy when the phone is used.

7 Which form of energy is stored in a battery pack?

8 Why are battery packs useful?

All electrical **appliances** include a circuit. As the electric current travels round the circuit in a radio, the loudspeakers transform electrical energy into sound energy. One way to describe energy transformations that take place in a device is like this:

type of energy put in $\Longrightarrow$ | device name | $\Longrightarrow$ type of energy coming out

For example:
electrical energy $\Longrightarrow$ | radio | $\Longrightarrow$ sound energy.

9 For each of the following, suggest a device that can carry out the energy transformation.

    a electrical energy $\Longrightarrow$ [   ] $\Longrightarrow$ thermal energy

    b electrical energy $\Longrightarrow$ [   ] $\Longrightarrow$ sound energy

    c electrical energy $\Longrightarrow$ [   ] $\Longrightarrow$ light energy

    d electrical energy $\Longrightarrow$ [   ] $\Longrightarrow$ kinetic energy

9I.2 How does electricity transfer energy?

The different parts of a circuit, such as bulbs, motors, loudspeakers and heaters, are called **components**.

As a current carries electrical energy round a circuit in a radio, it passes through the loudspeakers, which change this energy into sound. The current is not used up but returns to the battery to collect more electrical energy ready for its next trip round the circuit. When more current flows in the radio, more energy is carried from the battery. The sound from the loudspeakers becomes louder. An **ammeter** placed in the radio circuit will measure the size of the current flowing through that part of the circuit.

laboratory bulbs   *domestic lightbulb*

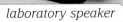
laboratory speaker   *Hi-fi speaker*

1 List <u>four</u> types of component.

2 An ammeter is placed in a radio to measure the current flowing through the loudspeaker. How does its reading change as the sound from a radio gets louder?

laboratory motor

washing machine motor

Simple circuits can be built as a single loop, called a series circuit. An example is the circuit found in a torch. Other circuits, called parallel circuits, are built with more than one loop. These include the circuit lighting a car's headlamps. In the parallel circuit, the current will divide between the loops (called branches), joining up at the far end. The total current in the circuit equals the sum of the currents in each branch.

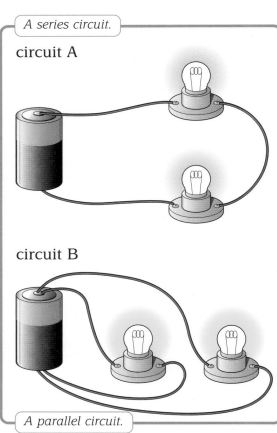

A series circuit.

circuit A

circuit B

A parallel circuit.

3 In a parallel circuit, the total current from the battery is 3 A. The ammeter in one branch of the circuit reads 2 A. What will the reading in the other branch to be?

Voltage makes the current flow round the circuit. A larger voltage forces more current to flow, carrying more energy. Batteries are labelled with their voltage. Car batteries normally have a voltage of 12.5 V because large currents are needed in the starter motor in the engine, but a watch uses a tiny current so its battery is only 1.3 V.

As the current passes through the circuit in the car, electrical energy is changed into **kinetic energy** and the voltage drops across the motor. Because there is a large energy change, the voltage drops a lot. Voltage is also called '**potential difference**'. A **voltmeter** is used to measure the difference in potential (voltage) on either side of components. In the car's engine, wires from the voltmeter are connected on each side of the motor, without breaking the circuit.

4 What happens when there is a larger voltage in a circuit?

5 Where is a voltmeter connected in a circuit?

A battery contains two (or more) cells joined together. The cells contain chemicals that react, producing a current when they are part of a complete circuit. The chemicals store chemical energy inside the battery. This chemical energy changes into electrical energy when the battery is part of a complete circuit.

6 What does the chemical energy in a battery change into in a circuit?

7 If a car battery loses 120 joules of chemical energy, how much electrical energy is transferred to the circuit?

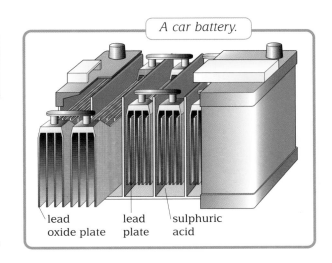
A car battery.

lead oxide plate · lead plate · sulphuric acid

A car battery contains lead and lead oxide layers with sulphuric acid in between. Smaller batteries commonly used in household equipment are called dry cells. The liquid acid found in car batteries is replaced in dry cells with different substances like pastes, which are less likely to leak and damage equipment. So dry cells do not need to be kept level.

8 Find out about the chemicals used in other types of battery.

Very high voltages are dangerous because of the large amounts of energy involved. When engineers work on high voltage transmission cables and **pylons**, or on electrified railway lines, the electricity travelling through the system must be switched off otherwise the engineers will be badly burned or killed. Sometimes, the voltages are so high that electricity can jump through the air to the nearest point connecting to earth. This happens in a thunderstorm when lightning strikes the highest point. This may be a tree or a tall building. In the same way, a person can get a fatal electric shock inside an electricity **substation**.

This tree was struck by lightning.

9 Why are high voltages dangerous?

10 A lightning conductor is a strip of metal on the side of a tall building. It is slightly higher than the roof and reaches the ground. How can the lightning conductor protect a building?

9I.3 Paying for and reducing the waste of electricity

Compare your home today with homes a hundred years ago. We now use many electrical appliances which can be plugged in and run from the mains supply. We use:

● lights instead of candles;

● electric cookers and electric heaters instead of open fires;

● TVs and music centres instead of playing family games;

● e-mails instead of writing letters.

Appliances such as fridges, washing machines and vacuum cleaners save many hours of housework. Each time you turn an appliance on, the electrical energy used is measured on your electricity meter and has to be paid for.

1 Write down <u>five</u> more appliances that use mains electricity.

The reading from this electricity meter is used to prepare your electricity bill.

Electric current from the mains supply carries electrical energy to components in each appliance where it changes into different forms of energy. The electrical energy is supplied at a high voltage (230 V in the UK), so a lot of energy can be supplied. Different appliances use up the energy at different rates. You will be pleased to hear that your CD player and TV use less energy per second than the vacuum cleaner, tumble dryer or cooker because they are less powerful. However, the longer the TV is left on for, the more energy is used up.

2 What voltage is mains electricity supplied at?

3 What <u>two</u> things affect how much energy an appliance uses?

The power of the mobile phone charger is shown in watts (W) on the rating plate (circled in blue).

It is possible to compare the energy used per second by examining a rating plate, which is found on most electrical items. The rating plate contains information about the voltage that the equipment works at, and its power. This is given in units of watts or kilowatts (a thousand watts). A watt is a measure of the amount of energy used by the appliance every second. It is measured in joules per second.

4 Write down the power rating of the mobile phone charger shown in the photograph.

5 Look at the table. List the equipment in order with the most powerful first.

Appliance	Typical energy used per second	Typical power
cooker	5000 joules	5 kilowatts
TV or computer	500 joules	500 watts
lamp	60 joules	60 watts
toaster	1200 joules	1.2 kilowatts

6 If a computer and lamp were each on for 3 hours, explain which one would add more to your electricity bill.

Some appliances transform nearly all the energy provided into forms of energy that we want. The percentage of energy transformed to the form we want is called the efficiency of the equipment.

Kettles are very efficient, and almost all the electrical energy provided is used to heat the water. Ordinary light bulbs are much less efficient. Only a small percentage of the electrical energy provided is changed into light, and the rest is turned into unwanted heat. Energy efficient light bulbs do not waste as much energy as heat, so more of the electrical energy changes into light.

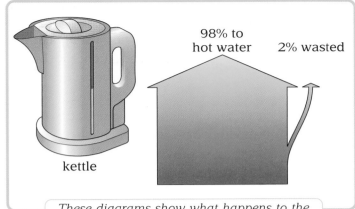

98% to hot water   2% wasted

kettle

These diagrams show what happens to the energy supplied to the appliance. The arrows show how much energy is turned into useful thermal energy, and how much is wasted.

7 What does efficiency measure?

8 Why do ordinary light bulbs use more electrical energy than energy efficient bulbs?

When energy is transferred, no energy is lost. However, it may not be in forms that we want, or be detected easily, or be reusable. All the energy transferred equals the original amount of energy provided. We say that the energy is conserved. Wasted energy is often unwanted sound or heat.

9 Name <u>two</u> common forms of wasted energy.

10 Write down the energy changes that take place in:

   a a light bulb;

   b a washing machine.

11 What forms of wasted energy are there when a light bulb and a washing machine are working?

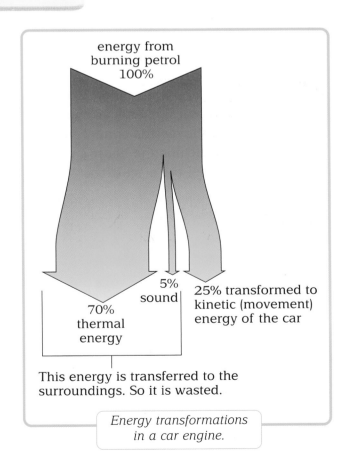

energy from burning petrol 100%

5% sound

25% transformed to kinetic (movement) energy of the car

70% thermal energy

This energy is transferred to the surroundings. So it is wasted.

Energy transformations in a car engine.

9I.4 Where do we get electrical energy from?

Mains electricity does not just appear at the socket in our walls but is generated first in a power station. In the power stations, energy from sources such as fossil fuels (coal, oil and gas), nuclear fuels, the wind, tides and water trapped behind dams is changed into electrical energy. An electric current flows from the power station, through the **National Grid**, to a substation and then to our homes.

Electricity pylons carry very high voltage electricity safely around the country.

The National Grid is a countrywide network of electric cables, supported by pylons, which links all power stations with substations. Substations are usually found in villages, and scattered through towns and cities. They change the very high voltages supplied by power stations into smaller, safer voltages for home use. Power cables in the street or buried underground carry the electrical energy from electricity substations to our homes. This way, our homes receive electrical energy safely from different power stations.

An electricity meter (often found under the stairs, or in the hall or garage) measures all electrical energy arriving at the house. Then the electric current travels through wires behind the house's walls before reaching the electric sockets.

Electricity substations contain transformers which alter the voltage.

1 What is the National Grid?

2 What does an electricity substation do?

3 Why do houses need electricity meters?

All that is needed to produce electrical energy is a magnet and a coil of wire forming part of a circuit. When either the magnet or the coil moves, a current flows in the circuit. This is because their kinetic energy is changed into electrical energy. The magnet and coil of wire are called a **generator** because they generate (create) an electrical current.

The current does not flow unless the coil or magnet is moving. This means that electrical energy cannot be stored. Instead, the energy is stored in the fuels and other energy sources that supply the power stations. If there is a surge in electricity demand, the power stations must supply more electrical energy quickly or there will be power cuts.

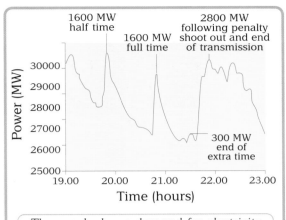

4 What does a generator do?

5 What energy change takes place in a generator?

There are many ways to make generators spin, even though they are massive and weigh several tonnes each. Most generators are connected to a turbine. A turbine has blades and spins when steam or air is blasted at it, just as a windmill's blades spin when it is windy. As the turbine spins, the generator spins too.

The steam is created by heating water in fossil fuel power stations and in nuclear power stations. The thermal energy needed is released when coal, oil or natural gas are burned, or when **nuclear fuels** split up into other substances and produce **radiation energy**.

The graph shows demand for electricity during the 1990 England–Germany World Cup semi-final. Surges in demand were caused by kettles and lights being turned on and water pumped when toilets were flushed.

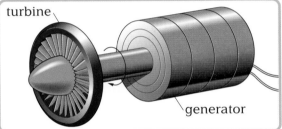

6 Why is a turbine used in power stations?

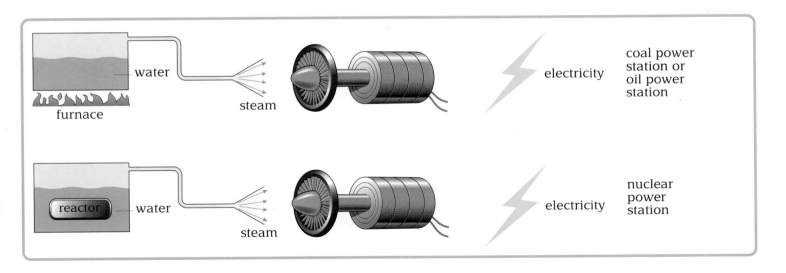

You should now understand the key words and key ideas shown below.

- Whenever anything happens, one type of energy is changed (**transformed**) into another type of energy or is **transferred** to a different place.

- Anything that changes energy from one form into another is called a **device**.

- **Chemical energy** is stored in fuels such as oil, coal and gas (**fossil fuels**), in food and in batteries.

- **Thermal energy** and light energy are released when candles are lit.

- **Potential energy** is stored when an object changes its shape or position.

- Electrical energy is useful because it can be changed into many other forms of energy and is convenient and clean.

- The different parts of a circuit are called **components**.

- A battery contains two (or more) cells joined together. The cells contain chemicals which react, producing a current when they are part of a complete circuit.

- **Voltage** or **potential difference** from a battery or the mains forces current to flow round a complete circuit.

- A larger voltage forces more current to flow. A **voltmeter** measures the size of the voltage.

- When more current flows, more energy is carried from the battery. An **ammeter** measures the size of the current flowing through it.

- If we add up all forms of energy transformed, it equals the original amount of energy provided.

- The electricity travels from a power station through the **National Grid** until it reaches an electricity **substation** where its voltage is lowered. Cables carry the electricity to houses, where it passes through an electricity meter before travelling through wires to electrical sockets and **appliances**.

- In a power station, a turbine spins a **generator** when steam or air is blasted at it, which generates electrical energy.

Gravity and space

In this unit we shall be discovering how gravity affects the way bodies move in space, and how our ideas of the Solar System have evolved. We shall learn about different types of satellite and their uses.

KEY WORDS
gravity
gravitational force
mass
kilogram
weight
newtons
constellations
orbit
satellite
geostationary orbit
low polar orbit

9J.1   What is gravity?

The force of gravity

Every time you jump, a force pulls you back to the Earth's surface. **Gravity** stops you floating away. Gravity is an attractive force (also called a **gravitational force**) between objects. Because of gravity, any object attracts every other object with a force. The size of this force depends on the size of the objects and their distance apart. Gravity tries to pull all objects on Earth towards its centre – of course, we never reach the centre because the Earth's crust keeps us at its surface.

Gravity is the reason that there is air trapped at the Earth's surface. Very few objects can escape the force of gravity: even birds, hot air balloons and planes fall back to Earth if they stop flying or burning fuel, and rockets need enormous thrusters to give them enough energy to leave the Earth's surface.

1   What type of force is gravity?
2   Where does a ball fall if it is dropped:
    a from a plane;
    b in Australia;
    c at the North Pole?

3   Two golf balls, placed near each other, do not roll together even though a gravitational force is attracting them towards each other. Why not?

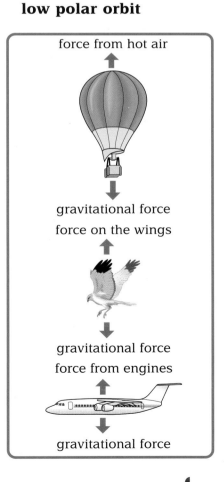

force from hot air

gravitational force

force on the wings

gravitational force

force from engines

gravitational force

Gravity and weight

Gravity acts between all objects because they have **mass**. The bigger the masses are, the larger the force of gravity between them. We say that objects with a large mass feel heavier, or have more **weight**, than objects with a small mass.

Weight is measured in **newtons**. Weight measures how hard gravity is pulling the object. One story says that Newton first thought about gravity when an apple fell on his head! The weight of an apple is about 1 newton.

Very massive objects have a gravitational force that is strong enough to attract all objects that are near their surface. Objects do not feel as heavy on the Moon because the Moon's mass, and therefore its gravitational force, is less than Earth's.

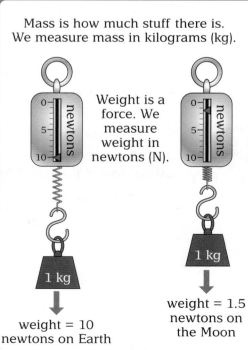

The force of gravity between two apples is very small. This is because they don't have much mass.

mass = 100g   mass = 100g

The force of gravity between an apple and the Earth is quite large. This is because the Earth has a very large mass.

mass = 100g

Earth

mass = billions of tonnes

4   What is:

   a mass;   **b** weight?

5   What are weight and mass measured in?

We call the area around an object where it will attract other objects a 'gravitational field'. This is similar to the area around a magnet called a 'magnetic field'. If you were to visit Jupiter, which is more massive than Earth, you would feel about three times heavier because its gravitational field is stronger than Earth's. Weight depends on the mass of the object and the gravitational field strength of the planet or moon it is on. In fact:

weight = mass × gravity
 (in N)   (in kg)   (in N/kg)

On Earth the gravitational field strength is about 10 N/kg. The weight of a kilogram bag of sugar is:
1 kg × 10 N/kg = 10 N

On Jupiter the gravitational field strength is about 27 N/kg so the same bag of sugar weighs:
1 kg × 27 N/kg = 27 N

Mass is how much stuff there is. We measure mass in kilograms (kg).

Weight is a force. We measure weight in newtons (N).

1 kg

weight = 10 newtons on Earth

1 kg

weight = 1.5 newtons on the Moon

6   What **two** things does weight depend on?

7   What is the weight of a 3 kg rabbit:

   a on Earth;   **b** on Jupiter?

Gravity from far away

The force of gravity between objects gets weaker as their separation increases. This means that the Earth's gravity still affects objects far away from its surface, but more weakly. To escape the effects of the Earth's gravitational field, you would need to be far, far out in outer space.

The Moon's gravity is felt weakly on Earth because the Moon is so far away and also because the Moon is smaller than Earth, so its gravitational field is smaller anyway. However, it is strong enough to move water on the Earth's surface, causing the tides. The Sun's gravity also affects these tides.

 8 What <u>two</u> things does gravity depend on?

 9 The Sun is much larger than the Moon, but it has less effect on the tides. Why?

Gravity and space travel

Rockets taking off from Earth can burn 13 tonnes of fuel in each second. This creates a force that thrusts the rocket up and away from the Earth's surface. As the rocket moves further away from Earth, its gravitational pull on the rocket gets less and so less force is needed to keep moving. The mass of astronauts inside the rocket does not change but their weight gets less as they move away from Earth. Rockets travelling to the Moon get a helping hand as they get closer because the Moon's gravitational field starts to attract the rocket, increasing its weight.

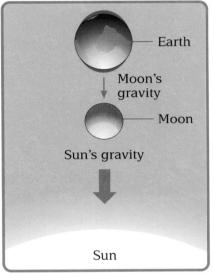

For space missions leaving the Moon, much less fuel is needed because the gravitational force is six times less than on Earth.

 10 An astronaut moves far away from the Earth. What happens to:

a her mass; **b** her weight?

 11 An astronaut moves closer to the Moon. What happens to:

a her mass; **b** her weight?

12 At position X on the graph, what can you say about the forces acting on the rocket?

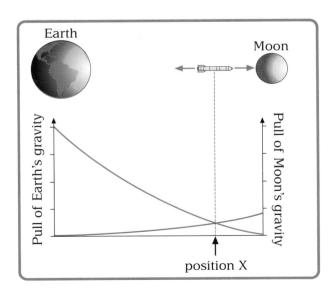

9J.2 How have our ideas about the Solar System changed?

Our understanding of the Universe has developed over thousands of years. Imagine being a scientist thousands of years ago. It was hard to write down your discoveries because paper was rare and few people could write. The best way to share discoveries was to teach or tell stories to other people. You could not talk easily to scientists from other lands because travel was hard.

Measurements could take years to make. Telescopes did not exist. People believed in many gods and feared the unknown. Cultural and religious beliefs are very strong and are passed down the generations. This often makes it difficult to persuade people that their beliefs might be incorrect even when there was good evidence. There have also been times when culture and religion were helpful to scientists and encouraged them.

Several thousand years ago, scientists could only observe. After a few thousand years, they had enough information to predict. As we get more information, our predictions and theories improve.

1 Write down <u>three</u> things that made scientific discovery hard thousands of years ago.

Early observations

Up to twelve thousand years ago, Stone Age people watched changes in the length of day and night. They recognised the seasons and years, and could plan planting and harvesting times for their crops.

A few thousand years later, the Egyptians recognised fixed patterns of distant stars arranged in a belt across a sphere (the sky). By 1600 BC, this belt of **constellations** was called the Zodiac belt. As they watched, they also noticed five wandering stars, which we now know were the planets. The Moon had a pattern of its own. It would grow to a full Moon, then dwindle till it was not visible and then become full again. Between 5000 BC and 4000 BC, the Egyptians developed the 365-day calendar.

The Pleiades

2 List the features in the sky that the Egyptians noticed.
3 What are constellations?

4 Why did the planets appear to move but the constellations seem fixed?

Early predictions

By 2000 BC to 1000 BC, Babylonians were able to predict the movement of the Moon and planets in relation to distant constellations, and created star catalogues. They could tell where the planets would be compared to the stars. They created calendars and predicted eclipses. About this time, Stonehenge was built in Wiltshire. Its stones line up with different positions of the Sun throughout the year, although the reason for its existence is not known.

It was 400 BC when Aristotle realised that the Earth was a sphere and not a flat shape (different stars could be seen from different countries). By 350 BC, sailors started finding their way at sea using the Pole Star. This was always visible from the seas that they were exploring in the Northern Hemisphere, but its height varied according to their position.

5 Why did Aristotle realise that the Earth was not flat?

6 Explain how sailors used the Pole Star.

Early explanations

The Greeks had many important ideas. In 450 BC, Philolaus thought that the Earth rotated and that the Earth, Moon and planets moved around a central fire. In 380 BC, Democritus realised that the Milky Way was made up from stars. However, Aristotle's ideas were believed more widely. By 390 BC, he taught that the Earth was at the centre of the Universe, and the Sun, Moon, planets and stars all moved around Earth, each held up by crystal spheres. He explained the movement of the planets using complicated arrangements that gave the right answers for the wrong reasons. Ptolemy published a book explaining Aristotle's ideas in 140 BC.

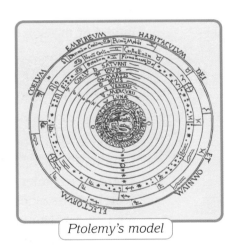

Ptolemy's model

The Roman Catholic Church also believed this theory. It was 1922 before the Roman Catholic Church officially believed the Sun was at the centre of our Solar System.

7 What did Aristotle believe was at the centre of the Universe?
8 What shape did Ptolemy believe the orbits were?

9 Which planetary object do you think the Greeks believed moved fastest? Explain your choice.

Changing models

Chinese astronomers made stone models of the Solar System in AD 1100, which correctly explained why solar and lunar eclipses occurred. Without telescopes, only five planets were visible and it was impossible to distinguish them from stars.

Centuries later, in 1543, Copernicus published a book stating that the Sun was at the centre of the Universe and that the Earth, Moon and planets travelled around it. This way, information gathered over many years made sense. This was the first description of the Solar System. He also discovered Saturn, the sixth planet.

In 1609, Kepler changed Copernicus' model slightly. Instead of circular **orbits**, he showed the shape of the planet's orbits as ellipses (ovals) and he also believed that their speed varied. Also in 1609, Galileo used the first telescopes to see craters on the Moon and details of the Milky Way. He also saw moons around Jupiter, which proved that all things do not orbit round Earth. He taught this to his students. This was a serious crime because it was against the Roman Catholic Church's teachings so he had to apologise publicly to the Church.

In 1781 William and Caroline Herschel discovered Uranus, the seventh planet, and in 1846 the eighth planet, Neptune, was discovered. It wasn't until 1930 that Pluto was discovered and the model of the Solar System that we know today was finally in place.

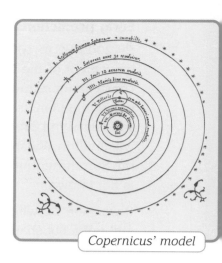

Copernicus' model

10 What is the main difference between Copernicus' model and Ptolemy's model?

11 How did Kepler's model vary from Copernicus' model?

12 Why were details of the galaxies not seen earlier?

There were many discoveries once telescopes allowed a detailed search of the skies, for example detailed star maps, features on planets, and comets. This topic only gives some information about a few important discoveries.

13 Choose <u>one</u> of the astronomers mentioned in this section. Find out more about them and make a poster about them. Include details such as when and where they lived, what discoveries they made, other important events that happened in their lifetime.

9J.3 What keeps the planets and satellites in orbit?

Why planets orbit the Sun

Imagine swinging a string with a stone tied to it, in a circle. The stone does not fly away because you are pulling on the string. The stone does not hit you because it is pulling the string tight. Now imagine that you are the Sun and the stone is Earth. The string shows the effect of gravitational pull between the Sun and Earth.

The Sun is massive. Its gravitational force is so strong that it can keep the planets moving around it. In the same way, planets also affect moving objects near to them. Because the Moon is close to Earth, it is Earth's gravitational pull that keeps the Moon in orbit.

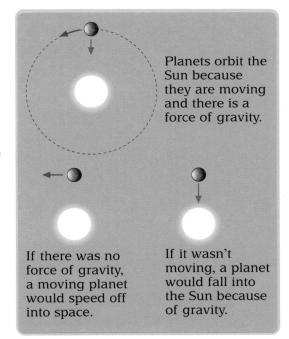

Planets orbit the Sun because they are moving and there is a force of gravity.

If there was no force of gravity, a moving planet would speed off into space.

If it wasn't moving, a planet would fall into the Sun because of gravity.

1   What would happen if:

    a there was no gravitational pull between the Earth and Sun;

    b the Earth was not moving near the Sun?

2   Which <u>two</u> things keep the Earth in orbit around the Sun?

3   What would happen to the Moon if the Earth's gravity did not pull on it?

Why satellites stay in orbit

A **satellite** is the name for a smaller object that orbits a larger one. Satellites can be natural (the Moon is the Earth's satellite and planets are the Sun's satellites) or man-made.

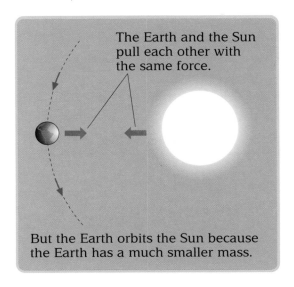

The Earth and the Sun pull each other with the same force.

But the Earth orbits the Sun because the Earth has a much smaller mass.

A satellite will only stay in orbit if it is moving at the right speed for the gravitational pull it feels. Satellites further away must travel more slowly than closer satellites. Man-made satellites have crashed to Earth because their speed was not right for their orbit.

The time it takes any planet to orbit the Sun is its year. Planets further away from the Sun have longer years. We can tell that they travel more slowly than planets close to the Sun by allowing for their longer orbits when comparing the length of their years.

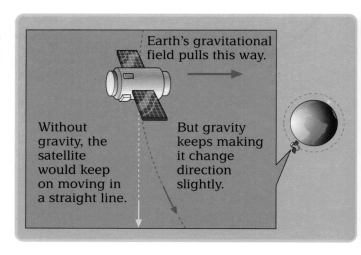

Earth's gravitational field pulls this way.

Without gravity, the satellite would keep on moving in a straight line.

But gravity keeps making it change direction slightly.

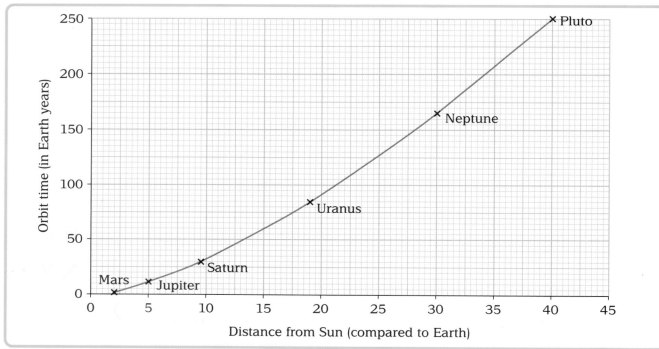

4   What do we call the time it takes a planet to orbit the Sun?

5   Explain how the graph helps to show that satellites far away travel more slowly than satellites nearby.

6   What force gets stronger as you get closer to the Sun?

Artificial satellites

The Russians launched the first satellite, Sputnik, in 1957. It was about the same weight as a man, and stayed in orbit for 57 days. Now, artificial satellites have many different uses and may be manned, or stay permanently in space. They are powered using solar panels, and have insulating blankets on their cold side. Satellites are often built of carbon fibre and aluminium, two materials that are strong but not heavy.

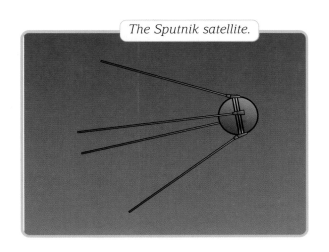

The Sputnik satellite.

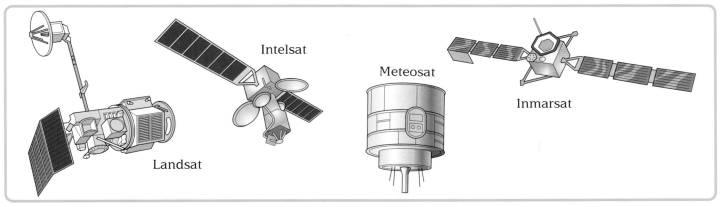

Intelsat

Meteosat

Inmarsat

Landsat

7 How many years ago was the first satellite launched?

8 Why must the materials used in satellites be light?

Different types of orbit

If a satellite is close to Earth, it travels fast and can make a complete orbit in 45 minutes. If it is further away, then it takes longer to orbit. One special orbit is called a **geostationary orbit**. The satellite stays above the same point on Earth all the time when it is in this orbit. A satellite in a geostationary orbit moves around the equator, in the same direction as the Earth and takes twenty-four hours to complete this orbit.

9 What is a geostationary orbit?

10 Is a satellite in a geostationary orbit closer or further from the Earth than one that orbits in 45 minutes?

Using satellites in geostationary orbits

Satellites in geostationary orbits can watch and communicate with the same part of Earth all the time. A satellite dish on a house receives signals from a satellite in a geostationary orbit. If the satellite shifted from this position, you would have to move your satellite dish, which would be inconvenient. Communications satellites are also in geostationary orbits. They are used for high-speed phone links, computer links and live television transmissions. Some weather forecasters use information from geostationary orbits. Because the satellite stays above the same place on Earth all the time, it can watch cloud movements change over a period of time.

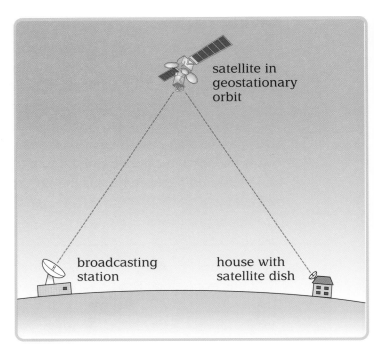

satellite in geostationary orbit

broadcasting station

house with satellite dish

 11 What are geostationary orbits used for?

 12 Why is it important that a satellite should stay over the same place all the time?

Using satellites in low polar orbits

Other weather satellites are put in an orbit very close to Earth. They can circle the Earth in 90 minutes. If their orbit is over the poles, then the Earth will spin under the satellite. This way, the satellite can scan the whole of the Earth's surface several times a day. This is called a **low polar orbit**. These satellites also produce computer images. These are used to study crops and forests, track oil slicks, forest fires and animal migrations, or look for places in the Earth that may contain oil or water reserves.

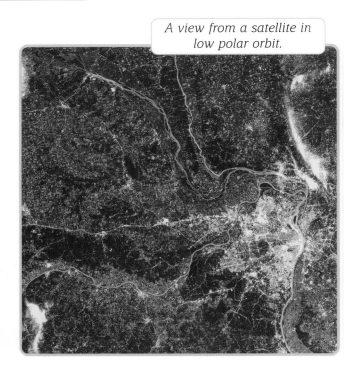

A view from a satellite in low polar orbit.

 13 Which parts of the Earth does a satellite in a low polar orbit travel over every time it orbits?

Other satellites

Large satellite telescopes can take photographs of the nearby galaxy, and can study the Sun in more detail. Since the orbit is outside the Earth's atmosphere, the photographs that are taken are much clearer than ones from any land-based telescope are, which have problems caused by clouds and lights from cities. The Hubble Space Telescope was launched in 1990 and since then has produced very detailed photographs of distant stars.

Satellites can be used to find the position of things accurately. The United States of America have created a global positioning system (also called GPS) by launching satellites in different orbits, each taking 12 hours to orbit the Earth. Anyone with the necessary equipment can use the system at any time and from anywhere in the world to find his or her position. It is accurate to 3 m.

The satellites are used for navigation, surveying, on the Space Shuttle and for many military uses. Aircraft and ships use GPS to help guide them during their journey and when approaching harbours or airports. Emergency vehicles, delivery vans and car drivers may use GPS to find their best routes and even farmers can use GPS to apply fertilizer and pesticides accurately.

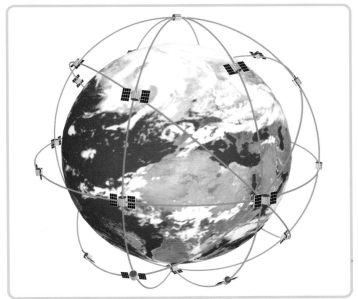

14 List <u>three</u> uses of GPS satellites.

15 Why would photographs of distant stars taken from Hubble be clearer than those taken from Earth?

You should now understand the key words and key ideas shown below.

- **Gravity** is an attractive force (also called a **gravitational force)** between objects.

- The size of a gravitational force depends on the **mass** of the objects and their distance apart: bigger masses have a larger force of gravity between them; masses a long way apart have less gravitational force between them.

- **weight** (in **newtons**, N) = mass (in **kilograms**, kg) × gravitational field strength (in N/kg)

- On Earth, gravitational field strength is about 10 N/kg.

- As a rocket moves away from Earth, the mass of astronauts inside the rocket does not change but their weight gets less.

- A **satellite** is the name for a smaller object that **orbits** a larger one. Satellites can be natural or man-made.

- A satellite will only stay in orbit if it is moving at the right speed for the gravitational force it feels.

- The time it takes any planet to orbit the Sun is its year. Planets further away from the Sun have longer years.

- In a **geostationary orbit** the satellite stays above the same point on Earth all the time and takes twenty-four hours to complete this orbit.

- Satellites in a **low polar orbit** can scan the whole of the Earth's surface several times a day.

- Large satellite telescopes can take photographs of the nearby galaxy, and study the Sun in more detail.

- GPS satellites can be used to find the position of things accurately. These satellites are used for navigation, surveying, and for many military uses.

Speeding up

In this unit we will study the idea of speed and the way forces affect how things move. We will also look at how streamlining is used to reduce the effect of water and air resistance. We will use the idea of balanced and unbalanced forces to explain how falling objects move.

KEY WORDS
speed
unit
acceleration
deceleration
streamlined
drag
terminal speed

9K.1 Describing how fast something moves

When we want to know how fast something moves we measure its **speed**. A **unit** tells you what something is measured in. The speeds of the car and the lorry have been measured in the unit 'metres per second'. We use the symbol m/s. For example, the speed of the car is 15 m/s.

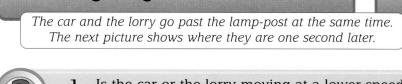

The car and the lorry go past the lamp-post at the same time. The next picture shows where they are one second later.

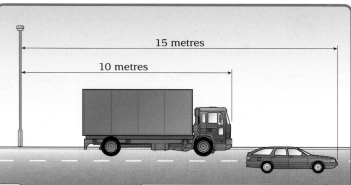

One second later. The car has travelled 15 metres. So, it has a speed of 15 metres per second. In the same time the lorry has only travelled 10 metres. Its speed is 10 metres per second. The car has a higher speed.

1 Is the car or the lorry moving at a lower speed? Give a reason for your answer.

2 What is the unit used to measure the speed of the car and the lorry?

3 What is the difference between the speed of the lorry and the speed of the car? Explain how you worked out your answer.

Different units

Metres per second can be a very useful unit for speed, but sometimes it is more useful to use a different unit. Road signs in Britain use the unit 'miles per hour'. Similar signs in France use the unit 'kilometres per hour'. The shorthand symbol for 'miles per hour' is 'mph'. The symbol for the unit 'kilometres per hour' is 'km/h'.

The speed of a tortoise walking across the floor is probably about 1 centimetre per second. We would write this as 1 cm/s.

4   What is the symbol for the unit 'kilometres per hour'?

5   Both photographs show speed limits of 40. The top photo is from Thailand and the bottom photo is from Britain. What is the important difference between the two?

6   Which speed is higher, 2 mm/s or 2 cm/s? Give a reason for your answer.

A fair comparison

In science most speeds are described in m/s. This means you can make a fair comparison between different speeds.

7   Which of the animals shown in the photos moves at the higher speed?

Speed = 30/ms

Speed = 20/ms

8   What do you have to do to make a fair comparison between the speed of a racehorse and the speed of a cheetah?

9   Find out the speed of light and what is special about it.

9K.2 Working out the speed

Sometimes you can get a direct measurement of speed from a measuring instrument that has been designed especially for the job. Police use radar guns and speed cameras to measure the speed of cars. People who study the weather use an instrument called an anemometer, which measures the wind speed.

1   Name <u>two</u> devices that give a direct measurement of speed.

2   What does an anemometer measure?

Timing things

If you want to compare the speeds of things that travel the same distance, you only need to measure the time they take. This happens in races since everyone runs the same distance.

3   Why can time alone be used to compare the speeds in an athletics race?

The timing method in the picture is the one used about 50 years ago. Today, the starting signal sounds from a small speaker behind each athlete. A clock is started electronically at the same time as the signal sounds. When the athletes cross the finish line, a camera linked to the clock registers the times. If two athletes pass the finish together, then the photograph from the camera is used to work out the winner. It is sometimes called a 'photo finish'.

Starting pistol   Timekeeper

Starter

4   What is different about the starting signal for an athletics race today and one about 50 years ago?

5   The person with the stopwatch used to start it when they saw the smoke from the gun, and not when they heard the bang. Why do you think this is more accurate than starting the watch when you hear the gun go off?

6   Suggest <u>two</u> reasons why electronic timing is better than using a stopwatch.

Calculating the speed

You calculate the speed of something from the distance it travels and the time it takes to travel that distance.

The swift has travelled 240 m in 6 s. Assuming the swift travels at a constant speed, you can work out its speed like this:

> speed = distance travelled ÷ time taken
>
> Therefore, speed = 240 m ÷ 6 s
>
> Therefore, speed = 40 m/s
>
> <u>The speed of the swift is 40 m/s.</u>

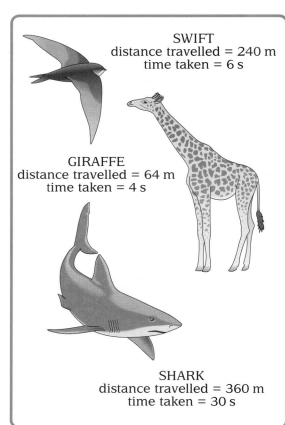

SWIFT
distance travelled = 240 m
time taken = 6 s

GIRAFFE
distance travelled = 64 m
time taken = 4 s

SHARK
distance travelled = 360 m
time taken = 30 s

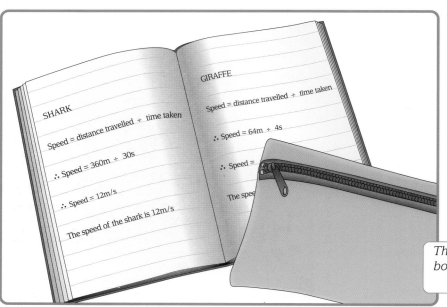

SHARK

Speed = distance travelled ÷ time taken

∴ Speed = 360m ÷ 30s

∴ Speed = 12m/s

The speed of the shark is 12m/s

GIRAFFE

Speed = distance travelled ÷ time taken

∴ Speed = 64m ÷ 4s

∴ Speed =

The spee

This drawing shows a pupil's exercise book where she worked out the speed for the shark and for the giraffe.

7 What formula do you use to calculate speed?

8 Which <u>two</u> measurements are needed so you can calculate speed?

9 If the pupil calculated the correct speed for the giraffe, what answer did she get?

Calculating distance and time from the speed formula

You can change the formula round to get other versions of it.

> time taken = distance travelled ÷ speed
>
> distance travelled = speed × time taken

For example, you find how long it takes a cyclist travelling at 20 kilometres per hour to travel 60 kilometres by using the version of the formula that starts with the time taken.

If you want to know how far a supersonic jet travels in 60 seconds at a speed of 500 metres per second, you pick the version of the formula that starts with the distance travelled. 30 000 m is the same as 30 kilometres. This means that a supersonic jet flying at 500 m/s travels 30 kilometres in a minute!

time taken = distance travelled ÷ speed
time taken = 60 km ÷ 20 km/h
time taken = 3 hours

distance travelled = speed × time taken
distance travelled = 500 m/s × 60 s
distance travelled = 30 000 m

10 Find the time taken for a swift flying at 30 m/s to travel a distance of 100 m.

11 Find the distance travelled by a car travelling at 22 m/s for 12 seconds.

Average speed

In the examples so far, we have assumed that the car, athlete, cheetah and swift all travel at a constant speed. This is not normally true. You do not usually stay at the same speed for every part of a journey. You can work out your average speed from the total distance you travel and the total time taken. So, our formula could have been written like this:

average speed = total distance travelled ÷ total time taken

When there aren't too many other cars about, you can travel at a steady speed along a motorway. This car travels 1500 metres every minute.

12 For the journey in the diagram, what is:

   a the total time;

   b the total distance;

   c the average speed in miles per hour?

13 Roger Bannister was the first athlete to run a mile in under four minutes. In 1954 he ran a mile in 3 minutes 59.4 seconds. A mile is 1609 metres.

   a Work out what Bannister's average speed was in m/s.

   b How long would it have taken him to run 1500 m at that speed?

   c Find out the current record for 1500 m and compare it with the time you calculated for Bannister.

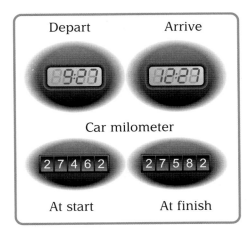

Depart	Arrive
09:28	12:28

Car milometer

27462	27582
At start	At finish

9K.3 Force and speed

If you want to change the speed of something, you need to apply a force. It is impossible to do an experiment on Earth to see how something would move with no forces acting on it. There is always a force of gravity acting on an object and there is usually also a force of friction to take into account.

A skater, gliding across very smooth ice, is about as close as you get in the everyday world to movement without friction.

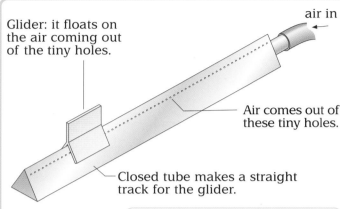

Glider: it floats on the air coming out of the tiny holes.

air in

Air comes out of these tiny holes.

Closed tube makes a straight track for the glider.

The force of gravity is balanced by the push of the air jets. These forces are also at right angles to the direction of the track so they have no effect on sideways motion. The cushion of air removes any friction between the glider and the track. The track must be set up so it is exactly horizontal.

In a laboratory you can set up experiments where the force of gravity does not affect the movement and where the force of friction is so small you can ignore it. An air track is a special device that will do just that. The only friction force when the slider moves along the track is the one produced by moving through the air. The glider is made of thin metal and card; it has a very small cross sectional area. This means that the friction force from the air is so small we can ignore it.

If you then sit the glider on the track so it is not moving, it will stay still provided all the forces on it are balanced and you do not give it a push. Once it is travelling, it is moving as if there are no unbalanced forces acting on it.

1   Which <u>two</u> forces always act on a moving object?

2   How is friction removed between the glider and the track on a linear air track?

3   What does the glider do if all the forces on it balance out and it is not already moving?

4 Why can the friction forces be ignored when the glider moves along the track?

Light gates are useful for measuring short times. When something blocks the light in the gate, the computer starts timing and it stops when the object leaves the gate and the light is no longer obstructed. If you use an object where you know its length, you can put that measurement into the computer and it will calculate the speed of the object for you from the length and the time the light is blocked. You can move the light gates to different positions but you keep getting the same result. The glider is moving at a constant speed.

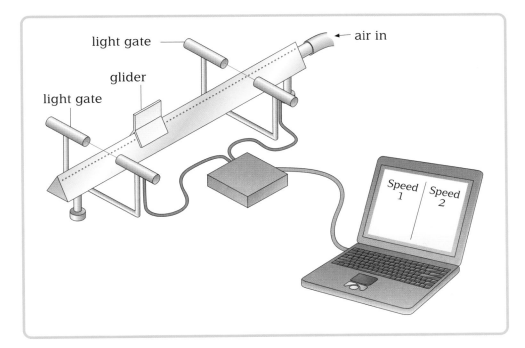

 5 What do the computer light gates do in the experiment?

 6 If the object is a card 3 cm long and it cuts out the light in the light gate for 0.7 s, how fast is it travelling?

7 What does the experiment show about how the glider moves when there are no unbalanced forces acting on it?

Applying a force

This time a piece of cotton with a washer on it has been attached to the glider. The pull of gravity on the washer provides a constant pull on the glider that is not balanced by anything. This table shows the type of results you get.

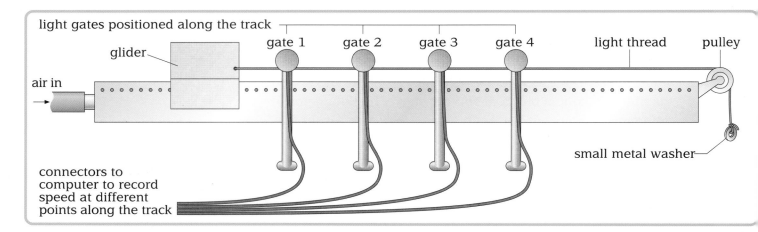

This time the glider is speeding up. We call this **acceleration**. An unbalanced force causes acceleration.

8 What does the washer do in the experiment and how does it affect the glider?

9 What does an unbalanced force do to the glider?

10 What do the results show is happening to the speed of the glider?

11 Find out what Newton's First Law of Motion is and what it has got to do with the results of this experiment.

	A	B	C
1	Speed at Gate 1	17 cm/s	
2	Speed at Gate 2	22 cm/s	
3	Speed at Gate 3	26 cm/s	
4	Speed at Gate 4	30 cm/s	

9K.4 Slowing things down

When an unbalanced force acts in the direction in which something is moving, it will speed the object up. If you make an unbalanced force act in the opposite direction to the one in which something is moving, the speed gets steadily less. We call this **deceleration**.

A simple way of showing this effect using a model car at home is shown in this diagram.

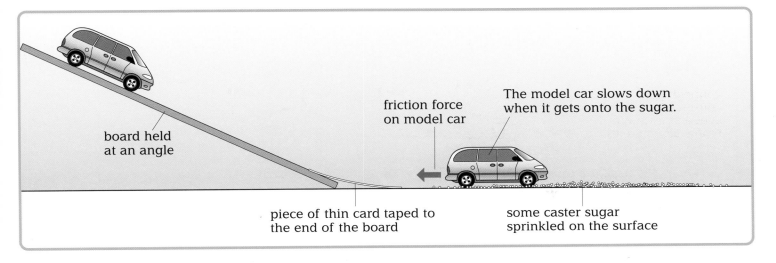

board held at an angle

friction force on model car

The model car slows down when it gets onto the sugar.

piece of thin card taped to the end of the board

some caster sugar sprinkled on the surface

The friction forces, in the opposite direction to the motion, slow the car down. If you sprinkle a few pinches of sand, salt or sugar on the worktop, the friction increases dramatically and the car will slow down much sooner.

1   If you apply a constant force in the opposite direction to the way something is moving, what will happen?

2   What does the word deceleration mean?

3   How can a track of gravel help to stop runaway cars at the foot of a hill?

A track of gravel is used at the foot of steep hills to stop cars and lorries that are out of control.

Keeping moving

If you have a car moving along the road, the wheels must supply a driving force to balance the friction forces or the car will slow down.

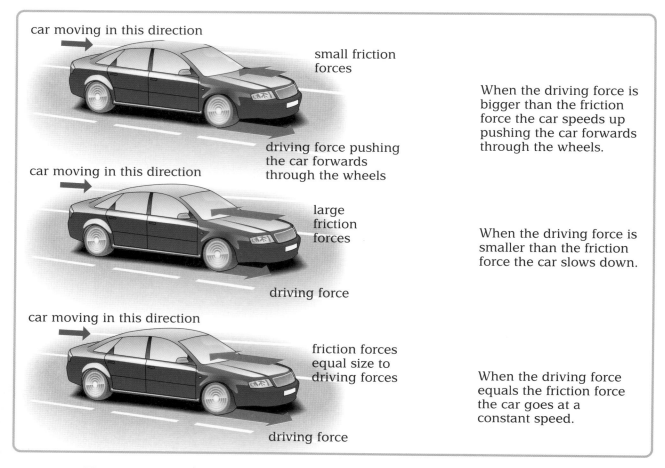

car moving in this direction

small friction forces

driving force pushing the car forwards through the wheels

When the driving force is bigger than the friction force the car speeds up pushing the car forwards through the wheels.

car moving in this direction

large friction forces

driving force

When the driving force is smaller than the friction force the car slows down.

car moving in this direction

friction forces equal size to driving forces

driving force

When the driving force equals the friction force the car goes at a constant speed.

The cyclist and the canoeist are both slowing down. In both cases the size of the driving force has dropped to zero, so there is only the friction force acting. The fish is swimming at a constant speed because the driving force from its fins is equal to the force of friction from the water.

4 What happens to a car when the driving force is bigger than the friction force?

5 What happens to a car when the driving force is smaller than the friction force?

6 What does the size of the driving force acting on an object have to be the same as for the object to move at a constant speed?

Using the friction force to slow down

You can slow something down if you increase the friction force. In a car the brakes do this. To find out about brakes and friction, see page 146 of the Spectrum 7 classbook.

7 Find out how planes landing on aircraft carriers are slowed down, so that they do not overshoot the deck.

9K.5 Streamlining

If you can reduce the friction force on a moving object, you can get it to go faster without making the driving force bigger.

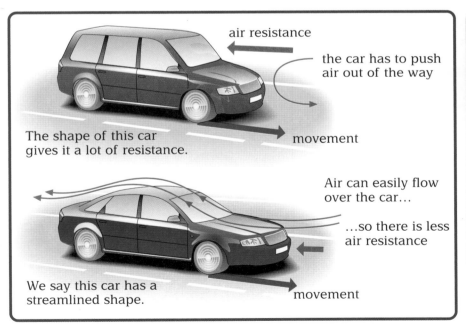

air resistance

the car has to push air out of the way

The shape of this car gives it a lot of resistance.

movement

Air can easily flow over the car…

…so there is less air resistance

We say this car has a streamlined shape.

movement

The idea of streamlining is used in racing cycle design:
- *smooth bodysuit*
- *shaved legs*
- *specially shaped helmet*
- *cyclist bent low*
- *no mudguards*

The red van needs a larger driving force. This is because its shape produces a bigger friction force from the air. The blue car has a shape that moves through the air more easily. We say it has a more **streamlined** shape. If the blue car and the van are the same weight and have the same size of engine, then the car will use less petrol than the van for the same journey.

The same idea applies to objects moving in water. Athletes in swimming competitions wear special swimsuits to reduce the friction in the water. Racing yachts are designed to keep friction forces to a minimum. You can show the effect of friction from water with a simple demonstration like this.

It takes a force of 3 N to pull this block of wood through the water.

A

It takes a force of only 1 N to pull this block of wood through the water at the same speed.

B

Block B has a more streamlined shape.

1 Why might the blue car use less petrol than the red van while travelling at the same speed?

2 Why do racing cyclists try to make themselves as streamlined as possible?

3 Why is it an advantage for a fish to have a streamlined shape?

The friction force depends on the speed

When you ride a bike the main friction force is **drag**. The word 'drag' is also used to describe the friction forces when something moves through air or water.

The petrol in a car is the source of energy for a car. Because the friction force is larger at higher speeds the car uses more petrol at 70 mph than it does at 30 mph. This table gives some typical figures.

Fuel consumption (miles per gallon)	Speed (miles per hour)
34	56
30.6	62
27.2	68

These figures are average figures for a car with all the doors and windows closed. If you drive along with an open sunroof or window, you will increase the drag of the air on the car and the petrol consumption will be higher.

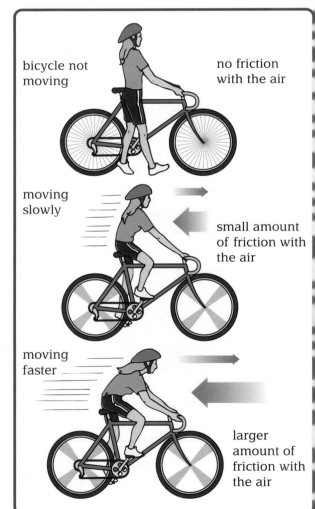

bicycle not moving

no friction with the air

moving slowly

small amount of friction with the air

moving faster

larger amount of friction with the air

4 What happens to the size of the drag on a car as it goes faster?

5 How does the size of the drag on a car affect the petrol consumption?

6 Why do racing cycles have handlebars or arm rests that allow the cyclist to lean forwards on the bike?

Friction warms things up

Friction forces produce a heating effect when surfaces rub against each other. You can see an extreme version of friction producing heat near 12th August every year. The Earth passes through the trail of dust in the orbit of the comet Swift-Tuttle. Particles of rock about the size of a grain of sand enter the Earth's atmosphere at a speed of about 60 kilometres per second! At this speed they collide with lots and lots of air particles as they pass into the atmosphere. This produces such a large drag force that the grains get hot and burn up. On a clear night you can see them burning. We call them shooting stars. This is known as the Perseids shower. It appears in the star constellation of Perseus. The first records of seeing it go back to AD 36.

You can use friction to light a fire.

Space capsules also get very hot as they re-enter the Earth's atmosphere. They travel in from space at high speed. The friction force produced heats them up to 2000 °C. The walls of a space capsule have to be very good heat insulators. They also need to be made of a material that does not melt or catch fire. It is important that the temperature inside the cone does not get above 40 °C.

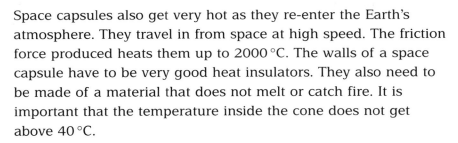

7 What do friction forces produce when objects rub together?

8 What causes a shooting star?

9 Why might it be important for the temperature of the interior of a space capsule to stay below 40 °C?

10 Find out when other showers of shooting stars can be seen apart from the Perseids.

9K.6 Skydiving and parachutes

Parachutes are mentioned in a Chinese text that dates from 90 BC. The first use in Europe was in 1793 when someone used one to jump from a hot air balloon over Paris.

Forces and terminal speed

The skydiver accelerates when an unbalanced force acts on her. As she steps out of the plane there is a force down on her due to gravity called weight. Because she has not started to fall there is no drag force to balance it so she starts to accelerate downwards. This is shown at point A on the diagram.

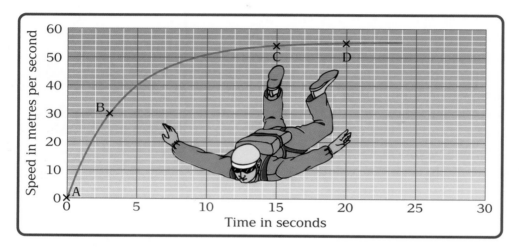

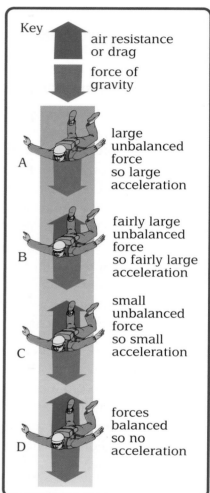

Key

air resistance or drag

force of gravity

A   large unbalanced force so large acceleration

B   fairly large unbalanced force so fairly large acceleration

C   small unbalanced force so small acceleration

D   forces balanced so no acceleration

At point B she is travelling at about 30 m/s. This produces a drag force which is smaller than her weight. This means there is still an unbalanced force accelerating her down but it is not as big as at point A. At point C she has almost reached **terminal speed** because the drag force almost balances her weight. The acceleration is very slight. From point D onwards the drag force balances the weight. She moves at a steady 55 m/s (125 mph). There is no more acceleration because there is no unbalanced force acting on her.

1   Which sections of the graph show where the weight of the skydiver is bigger than the drag forces?

2   Which section of the graph shows where the weight and the drag forces are balanced?

3   Explain why there is no more acceleration once the skydiver reaches a speed of 55 m/s.

Using the parachute

Parachutes use the drag force in the air to make things fall slowly. If the skydiver hit the ground at the terminal speed of 55 m/s, it would be terminal in more than one sense of the word. She would be killed! The parachute slows the skydiver down to a new terminal speed of about 6 m/s.

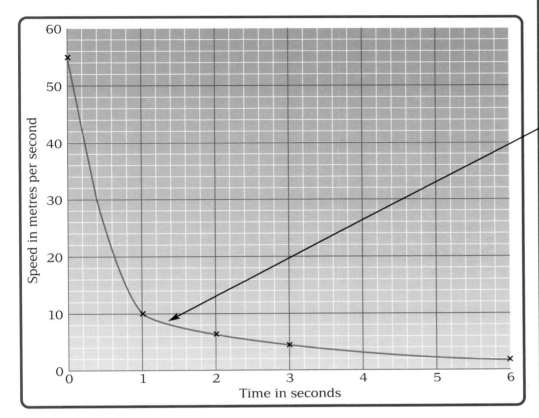

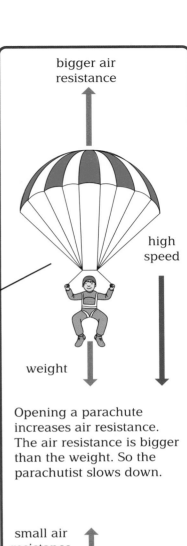

bigger air resistance

high speed

weight

Opening a parachute increases air resistance. The air resistance is bigger than the weight. So the parachutist slows down.

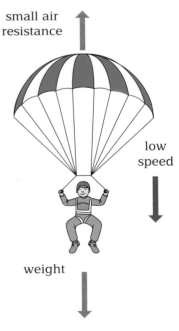

small air resistance

low speed

weight

Eventually the forces *balance*. The parachutist is falling at a lower speed.

4 What is the effect of a parachute on the terminal speed of a skydiver?

5 a Describe the overall force acting on the parachutist when the parachute has just opened.

b In which direction is this force acting and what effect does it have on the speed of the parachutist?

6 a Explain what the graph shape tells you when the parachutist is travelling at 6 m/s.

b What is the name for the speed at this point and what can you say about the forces acting on the parachutist?

7 Leonardo da Vinci described a working parachute in about 1480. Find out what his design was like and how it differs from a modern parachute.

You should now understand the key words and key ideas shown below.

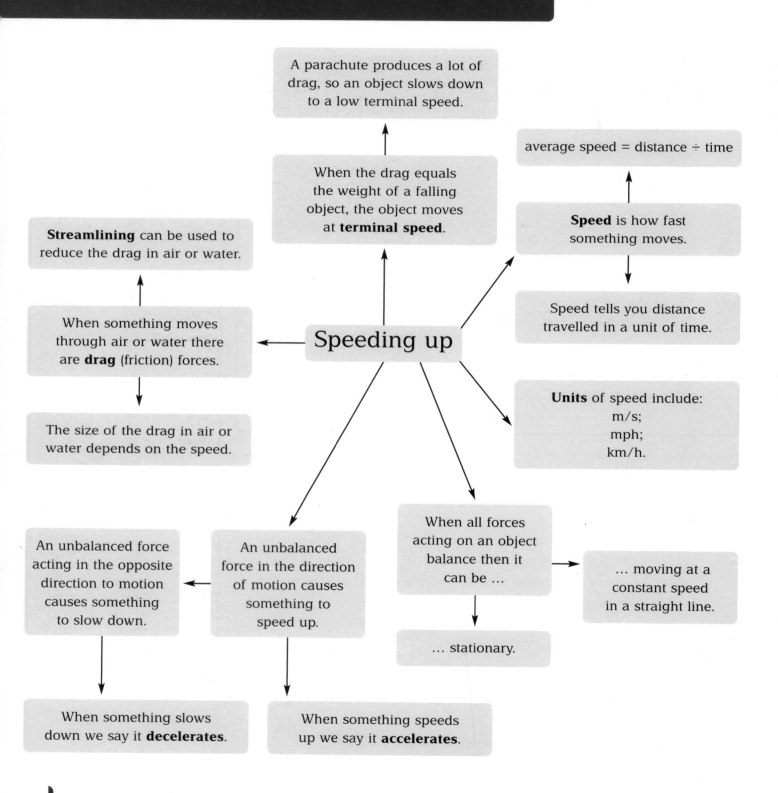

A parachute produces a lot of drag, so an object slows down to a low terminal speed.

When the drag equals the weight of a falling object, the object moves at **terminal speed**.

average speed = distance ÷ time

Speed is how fast something moves.

Streamlining can be used to reduce the drag in air or water.

When something moves through air or water there are **drag** (friction) forces.

Speed tells you distance travelled in a unit of time.

The size of the drag in air or water depends on the speed.

Speeding up

Units of speed include:
m/s;
mph;
km/h.

An unbalanced force acting in the opposite direction to motion causes something to slow down.

An unbalanced force in the direction of motion causes something to speed up.

When all forces acting on an object balance then it can be …

… moving at a constant speed in a straight line.

… stationary.

When something slows down we say it **decelerates**.

When something speeds up we say it **accelerates**.

Pressure and moments

In this unit we shall look at the effects of forces acting in two different ways, pressure and moments.

KEY WORDS
force
pressure
area
compress
pneumatic
molecules
gas
compressible
balanced forces
incompressible
liquid
hydraulic
moment
pivot
lever
load
effort

9L.1 What is pressure?

When a **force** pushes on a surface, it produces an effect called **pressure**. You apply pressure to the ground through the sole of your shoe for example. Pressure is a measure of how concentrated a force is on the **area** of the surface.

Applying pressure

The pressure a force produces depends on two things:

● the size of the force;

● the area it acts on.

If you press on the grass with your hand flat, you do not disturb the soil. But if you use a pointed stick to press with the same force, the point digs into the ground. This is because the same force acting on a smaller area produces greater pressure.

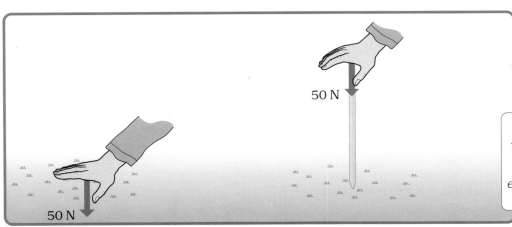

50 N

50 N

You can easily apply a 50 N push with your hand. This force is about the same as the weight of 5 kg bag of potatoes. The effect of a 50 N force depends on the area to which you apply it.

1 What <u>two</u> things does pressure depend on?

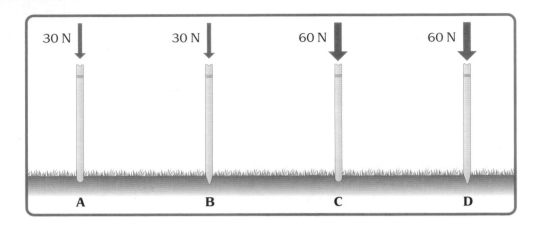

2 Look at the pictures.

a Which stump exerts the least pressure on the ground?

b Which stump exerts the greatest pressure on the ground?

c Which stump will be pushed furthest into the soil?

Using the pressure formula

If you know the force and the area, you can always calculate the pressure with the formula:

> pressure = force ÷ area

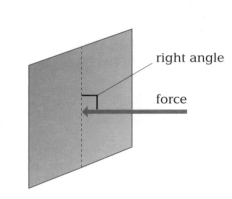

right angle

force

To use this formula correctly the area must be perpendicular (at right angles) to the force. For example, you can use this formula to find out which exerts a greater pressure, a force of 8 N on an area of 4 mm², or a force of 6 N on an area of 2 mm².

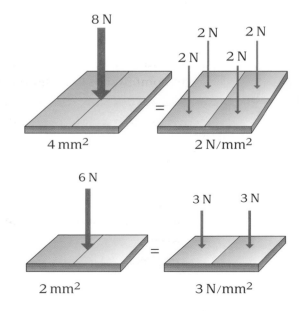

This diagram shows that the 8 N force is shared between 4 units of area.

A force of $8 \div 4 = 2$ N acts on each square millimetre. We say that the pressure is 2 N per mm² (N/mm²).

> pressure = 8 N ÷ 4 mm² = 2 N/mm²

This diagram shows that the 6 N force is shared between just 2 units of area. A force of $6 \div 2 = 3$ N acts on each square millimetre. We say that the pressure is 3 N per mm².

> pressure = 6 N ÷ 2 mm² = 3 N/mm²

Even though the 6 N force is smaller than the 8 N force, it exerts a greater pressure. This is because it is concentrated on a smaller area.

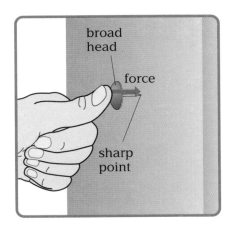

3 a Where is the pressure greater, on the head of the drawing pin, or under the point?

  b Explain why a drawing pin is designed with a sharp point and a broad head.

4 Explain why truck tyres sink into the mud, but tractor tyres do not.

5 Find the pressure for each of these combinations of force and area:

  a force = 10 N, area = 5 mm²

  b force = 20 N, area = 4 cm²

  c force = 55 N, area = 0.1 m²

  d force = 10 000 N, area = 2.5 m²

Pressure units

The unit of pressure is $1\,N/m^2$. This unit is given the name the pascal (Pa).

$$1\,N/m^2 = 1\,Pa$$

Pressure points

Sitting on a broad bicycle saddle is more comfortable than sitting on a narrow racing saddle. The broad saddle supports your weight over a larger area. Because the supporting force is spread out more, it applies a smaller pressure.

A

B

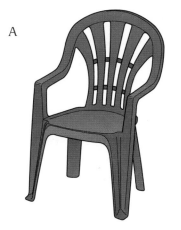

6 Explain why shaped chair seats are more comfortable than flat, hard seats, using the idea of pressure.

9L.2 Gases under pressure

Increasing pressure

A car driver uses a pressure gauge to check the air pressure in her tyres. If the pressure is too low, she pumps more air into the tyre. This will raise the pressure.

Air is a gas. It can be **compressed** (squeezed into a smaller volume) by applying pressure. A simple pump applies pressure through a moving piston. The piston compresses the air inside the cylinder. The increased pressure forces the air through the valve into the tyre.

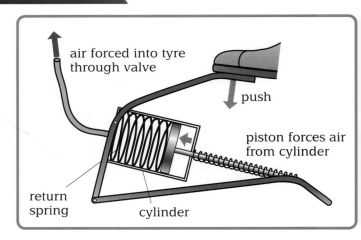

Machines that make use of gas pressure are described as **pneumatic**.

 1   What forces air into the tyre?

 2   The diagram shows pressure applied to a gas by a weighted piston. How will the piston move if half the weights are removed?

 3   What word describes machines that use gas pressure?

 4   Find out how an aerosol can, a water rocket, a peashooter and a steam engine use gas pressure to operate. In each case explain how the pressure is produced and how it is used.

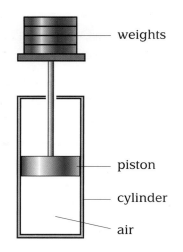

Moving molecules

The **molecules** in a **gas** are moving around at random in all directions and they will take up as much space as they have. So, a gas expands to fill its container. This means that gas molecules can be widely spaced apart, for example the average distance between air molecules in a room is about 10 times the size of a molecule.

There is plenty of empty space between the molecules. This means that molecules can be pushed closer together, and so a gas can be compressed into a smaller volume. We say it is **compressible.**

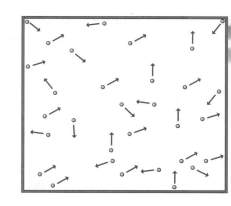

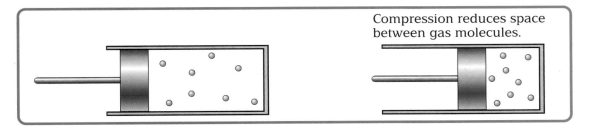
Compression reduces space between gas molecules.

5 Why can gases be compressed?

Pushing back

When you apply pressure to compress a gas, the gas pushes back with an equal and opposite pressure. This is an example of Newton's third law of motion. The pressure of the gas is created by the gas molecules as they collide with, and rebound from, the piston.

The gas molecules apply an equal pressure on all parts of the container walls. For example, the pressure of the gas inside an inflated beach toy keeps the wall stretched to give the toy its shape.

Gas pressure is increased when more molecules are added to the same volume. This is because more molecules collide with the container walls each second.

Newton's third law states:

For every force there is an equal force that acts in the opposite direction.

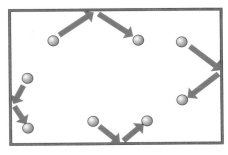
Molecules moving at random strike walls and rebound – applying pressure.

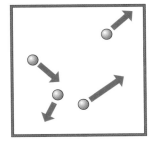
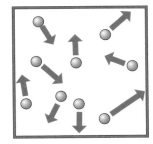

Gas pressure is also increased when a fixed amount of gas is compressed into a smaller volume. This is because the gas molecules are closer together, so on average they collide more frequently with each unit of area of the container walls.

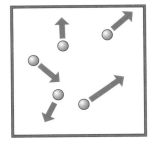

6 How do gas molecules apply pressure to the walls of their container?

7 Explain why pumping more air into an inflated football increases the pressure of the gas inside.

8 Explain why pressing down the plunger on a sealed syringe increases the pressure of the gas inside.

9L.3 Liquids under pressure

Incompressible water

A sealed plastic bottle filled with air and a second bottle filled with water feel very different if you squeeze them. The air-filled bottle squashes, but the water-filled bottle does not. Air compresses into a smaller volume when pressure is applied. Water is almost completely **incompressible**.

 1 Which bottle is more difficult to squash? Explain why.

 2 The forces applied to the pistons are increased.
   a Which piston moves?
   b Which piston does not move? Explain why.

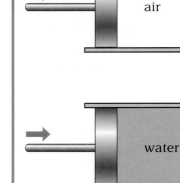

Crowded molecules

Unlike a gas, molecules in a **liquid** are crowded closely together. There is very little empty space between the molecules to close up when pressure is applied.

 3 Which diagram shows the molecules:
   a in a gas;
   b in a liquid?
4 Which sample is:
   a compressible;
   b incompressible?

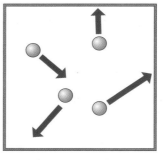

A

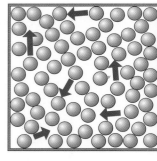

B

Under pressure

When pressure is applied to a liquid, the liquid pushes back with an equal and opposite pressure. The more pressure is applied, the more the pressure of the liquid rises. The pressure is the same at every point throughout the liquid. If it were not, liquid would move from high pressure to low pressure to even out the difference.

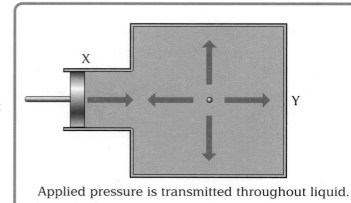

Applied pressure is transmitted throughout liquid.

 5 A pressure of $10 \, \text{N/cm}^2$ is applied at X. What is the pressure at Y?

Transmitting pressure

Water and other liquids can transmit pressure and forces from place to place. Look at the diagram. Yasmin applies a force to the plunger of syringe A. The force increases the pressure of the water in the syringe. The pressure is transmitted through the tube to syringe B by the water. To stop the plunger in syringe B from moving out, Eric must apply an equal but opposite pressure. Since the syringe plungers have the same area, the force required is the same.

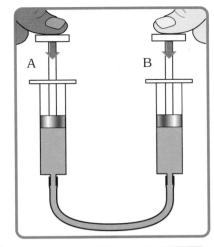

6   Yasmin applies a force of 5 N. The area of the plunger is 0.4 cm².

   a What is the pressure increase?

   b What force must Eric apply to balance this pressure?

Look at the picture. Aftab finds it difficult to stop plunger B moving because plunger B has a larger area. This means that a larger force is needed to produce the same pressure.

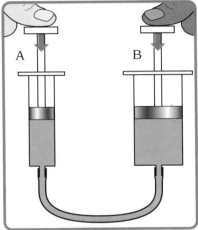

7   Which quantity, force or pressure, is the same throughout the liquid?

8   On which plunger, A or B, must the force be increased to produce the same pressure?

Hydraulics

Hydraulic systems use liquids to transmit forces. The hydraulic brakes in a car use hydraulic fluid (a type of oil) to transmit the pressure produced by the driver's foot on the brake pedal to the brake cylinders. Pistons in the brake cylinders push the brake pads.

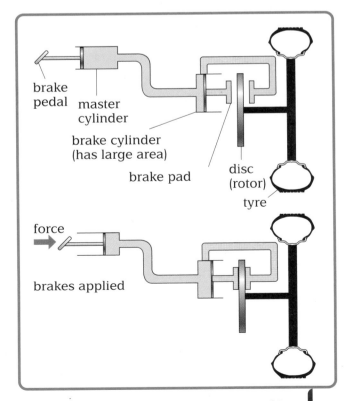

9   **a** Is the pressure in the brake cylinder different from the pressure in the master cylinder? If so, how?

   b How is the braking force produced by the brake cylinder different to the force applied by the driver's foot?

10 It is very dangerous if a slow leak allows air bubbles into the brake fluid. Explain why the brakes might not work properly.

Pressure and depth

If you dive under the water, you can feel the pressure on your ears increasing as you get deeper. At the surface the pressure is one atmosphere. The pressure under water is created by the weight of the water above pushing down. The pressure on a skin-diver 10 m down is 2 atmospheres, double the pressure at the surface.

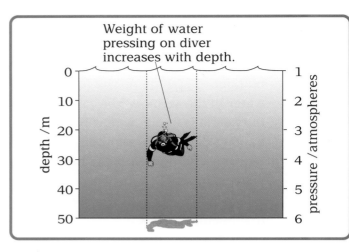
Weight of water pressing on diver increases with depth.

11 What is the pressure at a depth of 50 m?

12 Why is it dangerous for a submarine to dive below the maximum depth for which it is designed?

13 Explain how this demonstration shows that pressure changes with depth in a liquid.

9L.4 Turning forces

Making things turn

You need to push or pull to open this door. The door pivots on hinges at one side, so the force does not move the door in a straight line. The force makes the door turn. The turning effect of a force is called its **moment**.

1 What do we call a turning effect caused by a force?

turning effect of force

force

Clockwise and anticlockwise moments

The weight of the boy produces a clockwise turning force on the seesaw. The moment of the boy's weight turns the seesaw in the same direction as the hands on a clock. The weight of the girl turns the seesaw in the opposite direction. It produces an anticlockwise moment.

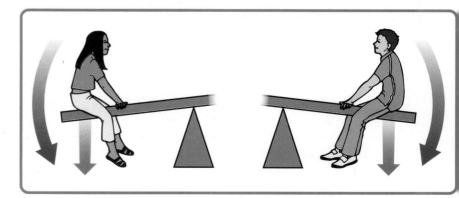

2 The diagrams show some more forces with moments around pivots. In each case, state which way the object will turn.

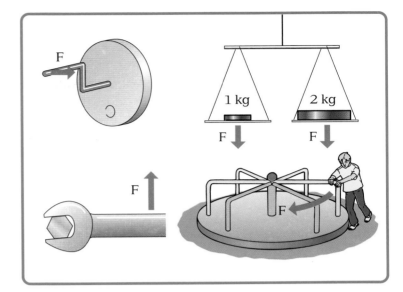

Changing the moment

The size of a turning moment depends on two things:

- the size of the force;
- its distance from the **pivot**.

It is easier to open a door if you push as far from the hinge as possible. The same force applied further from the hinge has a bigger moment.

3 What <u>two</u> things does the size of a moment depend on?

4 Which force, A, B or C, produces the greatest moment on the door?

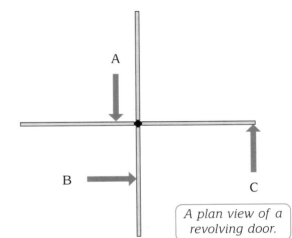

A plan view of a revolving door.

A spanner provides a moment to undo a nut. If the nut is too tight, you can increase the turning effect of the force by using a longer spanner.

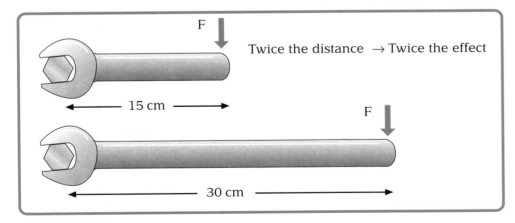

Twice the distance → Twice the effect

15 cm

30 cm

5 What are the <u>two</u> ways you can increase the turning effect of a spanner on a nut?

6 How can you make a moment smaller? Give <u>two</u> ways.

Body levers

Your arms and legs are **levers**. Your joints are
pivot points. Your muscles make your limbs bend
by producing turning forces around your joints.
Muscles apply forces by contracting. They can
only pull, not push. So you need a pair of muscles
to operate your limbs at each joint. One muscle to
bend, the other to straighten. The muscle that
bends your arm at the elbow is the biceps. The
muscle that straightens it again is the triceps.

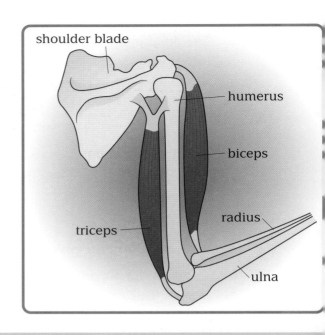
shoulder blade
humerus
biceps
triceps
radius
ulna

7 Name <u>two</u> parts of your body that act as:

 a levers;   **b** pivots.

Calculating moments

To use this formula correctly, the force must
be at right angles to the line from the pivot
to the place where the force acts.

You can work out a moment with this formula:

moment = force × distance of force from pivot

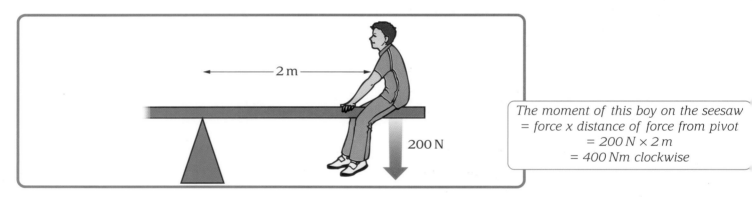

2 m

200 N

*The moment of this boy on the seesaw
= force × distance of force from pivot
= 200 N × 2 m
= 400 Nm clockwise*

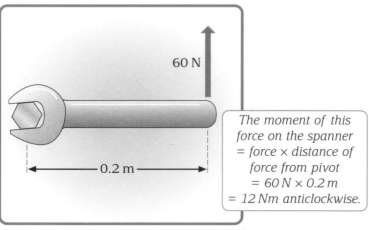

60 N

0.2 m

*The moment of this
force on the spanner
= force × distance of
force from pivot
= 60 N × 0.2 m
= 12 Nm anticlockwise.*

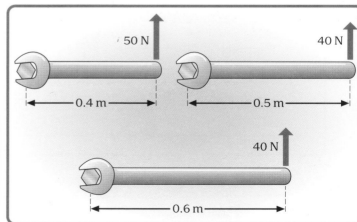

50 N

40 N

0.4 m

0.5 m

40 N

0.6 m

8 Find the moments in each of these examples. Which
spanner produces the biggest moment on the nut?

9L.5 Balance and levers

Balancing a seesaw

A smaller person can balance a larger person on a seesaw by sitting further from the pivot. We can use moments to explain how balance works.

The weight of the smaller person in the example produces an anticlockwise moment.

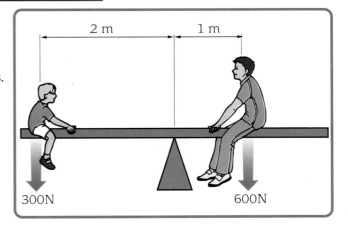

anticlockwise moment = weight A × distance A
$$= 300\,N \times 2\,m$$
$$= 600\,N\,m$$

The weight of the larger person produces a clockwise moment.

clockwise moment = weight B × distance B
$$= 600\,N \times 1\,m$$
$$= 600\,N\,m$$

To be in balance, the anticlockwise moment must equal the clockwise moment.

anticlockwise moment = clockwise moment
weight A × distance A = weight B × distance B
$$300\,N \times 2\,m = 600\,N \times 1\,m$$

From this formula we can see that because person A is just half the weight of person B, he must sit twice as far from the pivot to produce the same size moment.

This balance formula is called the principle of moments. The principle states that balance is achieved when:

anticlockwise moment = clockwise moment

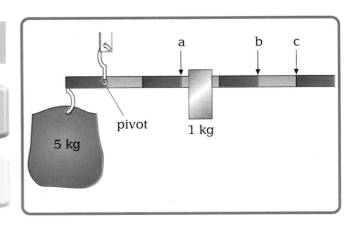

1 What must happen for a seesaw to balance?

2 Where must you position the weight to balance the load on this beam balance?

Balanced machines and bodies

A tower crane must be kept in balance when it lifts a **load**, or it will topple over. The load on this crane produces a clockwise moment about the top of the tower. This is balanced by a counterweight that produces an anticlockwise moment

 3 What do cranes use to remain balanced when they lift loads?

 4 Which way must the counterweight be moved after the crane driver has released this load? What would happen if the counterweight were not shifted?

The weight can be shifted towards or away from the tower to maintain balance when the crane lifts different size loads.

As the gymnast leans forward, her upper body produces an anticlockwise moment about her foot (the balance point). She produces a balancing clockwise moment by extending her free leg in the opposite direction.

 5 Use moments to explain why the counterweights must be present when the truck lifts a load.

They may not realise it, but when dancers and gymnasts balance, they are using the principle of moments.

 6 How do gymnasts use the principle of moments to remain balanced?

Levers

A lever is a simple machine that uses moments to apply and change forces. This girl is applying a force (called an **effort**) at one end of the lever to lift a weight (called a load) on the other side of the pivot.

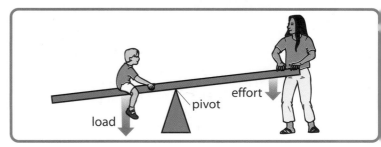

The principle of moments shows how the girl can use a small effort to lift a larger load. She must apply the effort further from the pivot than the load.

principle of moments applied to a lever:

effort × distance from effort to pivot = load × distance from load to pivot

A lever used in this way increases the effort. We say levers <u>magnify</u> effort. But you never get something for nothing! If the lever increases the force, then the distance moved is decreased. The girl pushes through a large distance to lift the toddler a small distance.

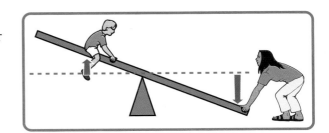

7 **a** What does a lever magnify?

  b How does the lever do this?

8 Use a ruler to measure the effort to pivot and load to pivot distances on the nail extractor. Use your measurements and the principle of moments to calculate how many times it magnifies the effort.

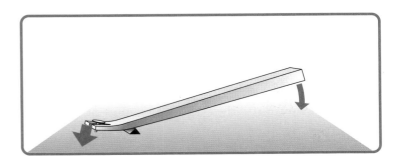

Magnifying distance

People also use levers to magnify distance. For example a long fishing rod converts a small movement of the hands to a large movement of the rod tip.

A rowing oar is another example of a lever used in this way.

9 Look at the picture of the rower.

  a Identify the objects that are the effort, pivot and load in this diagram.

  b Which force is greater, the effort or the load?

  c Which moves further, the effort or the load?

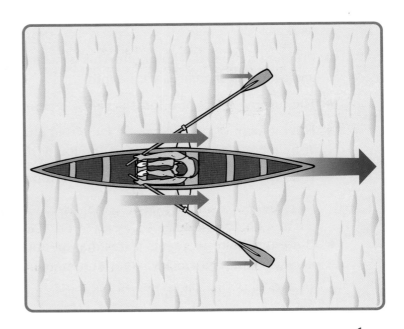

You should now understand the key words and key ideas shown below.

- **Pressure** is the effect of a **force** acting on an **area**. Pressure can be increased either by increasing the force or by decreasing the area.

- Pressure can be calculated from the formula:

  pressure = force ÷ area

- The SI unit of pressure is the newton per square metre (N/m^2). This unit is called the pascal (Pa).

  $1\,N/m^2 = 1\,Pa$

- **Gas** pressure is produced by gas **molecules** colliding with the container walls, and with anything in the gas.

- A gas is **compressible**. It can be squeezed into a smaller volume by increasing the pressure on it.

- **Pneumatic** describes the action of machines that use gas pressure to work.

- A **liquid** is **incompressible**, it cannot be squeezed into a smaller volume.

- Applied pressure is transmitted throughout a liquid or a gas inside a container.

- **Hydraulic** describes the action of machines that use liquid pressure to work.

- Pressure increases with depth. This is because the weight of the liquid or gas overhead increases with depth.

- The turning effect of a force is called its **moment**.

- The moment of a force can be increased either by increasing the force, or by increasing the distance of the force from the turning point (**pivot**).

- The moment of a force can be calculated from the formula:

  moment = force × distance of force from pivot

- The principle of moments states that an object is balanced when clockwise and anticlockwise turning moments are equal.

- A **lever** uses the principle of moments to amplify the force, or the distance moved, when an **effort** is used to move a **load**.

Scientific investigations

Throughout this course you have looked at investigations carried out by scientists, past and present, and have done your own investigations. In Years 7 and 8 you learnt and used these investigation skills:

- finding suitable questions for investigations;

- choosing the best strategy for an investigation;

- planning investigations, including choosing a suitable range of readings;

- presenting results, including using computers to collect data and present results;

- using scientific ideas in conclusions;

- evaluating the strength of evidence.

This chapter will help you to improve your skills still further.

KEY WORDS
preliminary tests
relevant
reliable
accurate
validity of results
evidence
opinions
biased

Using preliminary work such as trial runs

Scientists often do trial runs of experiments to find out whether their approach will work or not. You probably used trial runs in 8H in the investigation of the composition of limestone.

Mrs Tasker asked her class to find out which of three varieties of apples gave the most juice. One way of doing this is to find out how much of each apple is water. She set her class some preliminary work using books to research a way of finding out how much of an apple is water. No one found that actual experiment, but Bryan found one about the amount of water in soil. Using the same idea, he suggested an experiment:

- Find the mass of an apple.

- Heat it to get rid of all the water.

- Find its mass again. The loss in mass will be equal to the mass of water that was in the apple.

Anna found out that you needed to repeat this several times until two masses were the same. It is called heating to constant mass and you do it so you can be sure that all the water has gone. Lee thought that chopping the apple might make drying faster.
Mrs Tasker was pleased with the ideas so far – but she pointed out that they hadn't described how to heat the apple.

She suggested that they needed to do some **preliminary tests**. They needed to try out their ideas to find out which one worked best.

1   What <u>two</u> kinds of preliminary work did the class do before they planned their investigation?

	Heat over Bunsen flame		Dry on an open shelf at 20 °C		Heat in an oven at 100 °C		Heat in an oven at 300 °C	
Size of apple pieces	cut into 1/8ths	chopped up small	cut into 1/8ths	chopped	cut into 1/8ths	chopped up small	cut into 1/8ths	chopped up small
Mass at start (g)	140.8	136.4	142.3	143.5	138.6	136.7	133.6	139.1
Mass after 40 mins (g)	12.7	10.1	137.6	135.2	103.5	100.8	10.9	10.1
Mass after 1 day (g)	not done	not done	69.1	67.7	17.3	16.2	9.4	8.4
Mass after 7 days (g)	not done	not done	28.5	28.9	17.3	16.2	not done	not done
Loss in mass (g)	128.1	126.3	113.8	114.6	121.3	120.5	124.2	130.7
% loss in mass	91	92.5	80	80	87.5	88	93	94
Observations	black (burnt)	black (burnt)	brown and mouldy	brown and mouldy	brown	brown	black (burnt)	black (burnt)

Results of preliminary tests.

2 The pupils rejected heating over a Bunsen and in an oven at 300 °C because the apple lost more than just water.

   a What evidence is there that more than just water was lost?

   b Suggest what else was lost.

3 Suggest <u>two</u> problems of drying the apple at 20 °C.

4 These tests didn't show whether chopping up the apple made a difference to the time taken to dry the apple. What extra tests can the class do to find out the answer?

5 In the final plan for their investigation, why did the pupils:

   a chop up the apples;

   b find the mass of the apples on a digital balance;

   c heat in an oven at 100 °C;

   d heat to constant mass?

6 Write a list of other ideas that the pupils probably used to make their investigation safe and their results valid.

Improving the validity of results

You already know that it is important to:

- choose a suitable design of your investigation to ensure that your evidence is **relevant**. Relevant evidence is evidence that will help you to answer your question.

- record sufficient observations or readings to ensure that your evidence is **reliable**.

- choose suitable measuring instruments and take accurate and precise readings to ensure that your evidence is **accurate**.

So, the **validity of results** depends on the accuracy and precision of the <u>measuring instruments</u> that you choose and <u>how well you use them</u>.

Tanya wanted to investigate how the concentration of acid affects the volume needed to neutralise an alkaline solution. She needed to measure the volumes of water and acid accurately to get the concentration that she wanted. Tanya's teacher asked her to compare three different ways of measuring $10\,cm^3$ of water. $10\,cm^3$ of water should have a mass of $10\,g$, so her teacher suggested that Tanya could check the accuracy of the measurements by finding the mass of each $10\,cm^3$ of water on an accurate balance.

7 Why did Tanya take so many readings?

8 What was the range of measurements using <u>each</u> of the three instruments?

9 Why did the measurements using the $10\,cm^3$ measuring cylinder vary?

10 a Which instrument was the least accurate of the three?

   b Suggest why.

11 The average mass of water for all the instruments was below the expected $10\,g$. Suggest some reasons for this.

12 Apart from the accuracy of the instruments, what else affects the accuracy and precision of this set of results?

13 What lessons can you learn from Tanya's results?

Tanya found the mass of a container (70 g), then found its mass again with the water in (79.90 g).

Mass of water (g) using		
$10\,cm^3$ measuring cylinder	$100\,cm^3$ measuring cylinder	$10\,cm^3$ pipette
9.80	9.50	9.90
9.88	8.90	10.01
9.74	9.83	9.88
9.97	10.12	9.83
9.97	9.75	9.96
9.83	9.70	9.92
9.84	9.05	9.97
9.85	8.75	9.84
9.86	9.24	9.77
9.87	9.25	9.89

Tanya's results

Choosing the best ways of presenting results

Rannoch decided to investigate how the melting point of wax varies for different types of wax. In his preliminary work, he heated a sample of candle wax to 100 °C in a water bath. As the wax then cooled, he measured its temperature every minute.

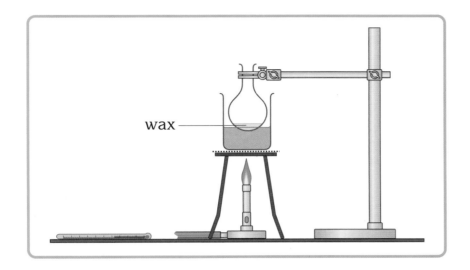

Time (minutes)	Temperature (°C)
0	80
1	74
2	68
3	65
4	62
5	60
6	59
7	58
8	57
9	57
10	57
11	57
12	57
13	57
14	56
15	55
16	53
17	50
18	47
19	44
20	41

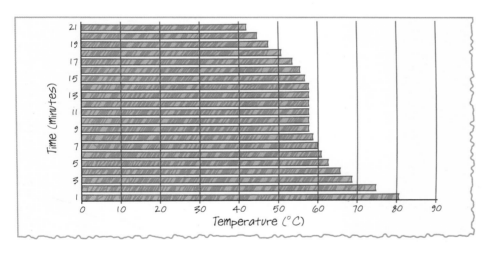

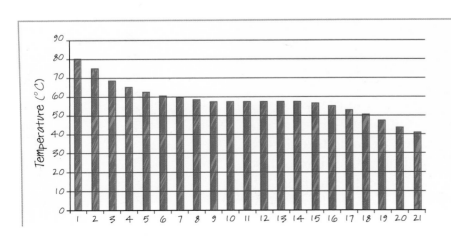

Rannoch plotted these results in a series of charts and graphs to help him find a pattern to his results.

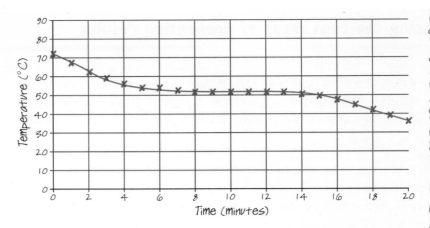

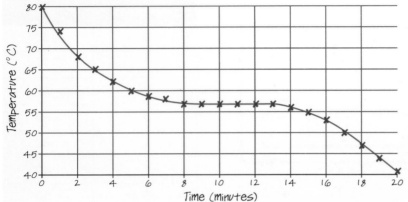

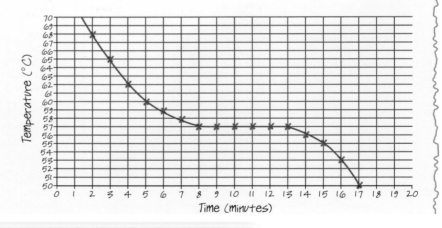

14 Chart A is not the correct type of chart to draw for this data. Why not?

15 Is Chart B suitable for this data? Explain your answer.

16 Graph C does not display the results very clearly. Why not?

17 Which graph shows the melting point most clearly, Graph D or Graph E? Explain your answer.

18 Rannoch's teacher suggested that he could take the temperature readings every half minute for part of his experiment. Between which times would it be most important to take the temperature every half minute?

19 What else would improve the accuracy of his results?

Interpreting patterns in data and checking reliability, making predictions

Valerie's class had been studying how forces made objects accelerate. Valerie decided to investigate how the mass of a trolley affected its acceleration. She designed an experiment to test her prediction.

Rather than measuring the acceleration, Valerie decided to measure the speed after the trolley had travelled 30 cm. The greater the acceleration, the greater the speed. She measured the speed 3 times for each mass.

Here is Valerie's prediction:

> I predict that as I increase the mass of the trolley, then its acceleration will decrease.

Mass of Trolley (kg)	Speed after 30 cm (m/s)			
	1	2	3	Ave
0.5	2.49	2.47	2.43	2.46
1	1.73	1.74	1.76	1.74
1.5	1.43	1.89	1.41	1.58
2	1.22	1.21	1.24	1.22
2.5	1.15	1.1	1.09	1.11
3	1.1	1.01	0.99	1.03
3.5	0.93	0.94	0.99	0.95
4	0.61	0.87	0.87	0.78
4.5	0.81	0.89	0.81	0.84
5	0.77	0.79	0.75	0.77

Valerie's results

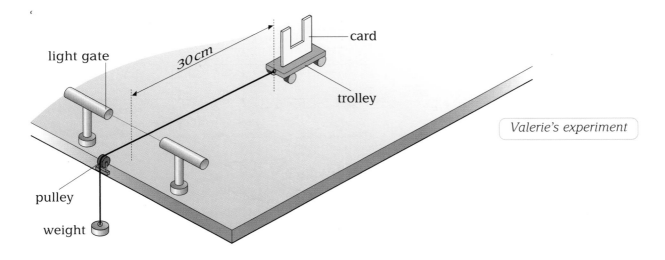

Valerie's experiment

20 Look at this table of data, are there any readings which are obviously inaccurate? If so, which ones?

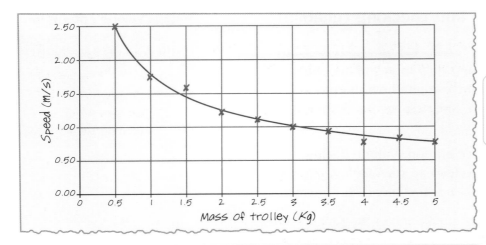

Valerie plotted her results for average acceleration. She put a line of best fit through the points. It was a curve.

21 What happens to the speed of the trolley after 30 cm when the mass is increased?

22 What happens to the acceleration of the trolley as the mass is increased?

23 Was Valerie's prediction correct?

24 Use the graph to predict what the speed of the trolley would be when there is a mass of 1.7 kg.

25 How could you check your answer to question 24?

26 Which points on the graph do not fit on the line of best fit?

Valerie was not happy that some of the points did not fit exactly on the line of best fit. She decided to plot all of her readings on the graph rather than the averages. Using this method she could check to see which of her results were less reliable.

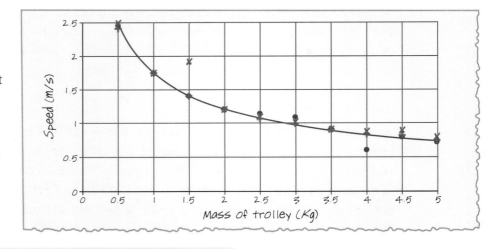

27 Use this graph to identify which readings are the least accurate.

28 What could Valerie now do to make her average speeds more accurate?

Looking at evidence

Measurement and observation are part of the process of collecting **evidence** to support an explanation or theory. You need to be able to look at evidence and decide:

- whether there is enough evidence to support a conclusion. You looked at that in Years 7 and 8 and in the evaluation of your own investigations;

- whether or not things presented as evidence are <u>actually evidence</u>.

In your research about reproduction, you may have come across the idea that sperm contain a 'miniature human'. Several scientists claimed to have seen this 'homunculus' in sperm cells. It is probably a matter of one scientist's interpretation of a fuzzy image being taken up by others. They may have imagined what they saw, seen what they expected or wanted to see, or just not wanted to admit that they couldn't see anything. So, descriptions of a 'homunculus' were <u>not</u> evidence of anything. Perhaps you have said that you could see something under a microscope when you weren't really sure!

Sometimes people give their **opinions**. They say what they think, with no evidence for their ideas. Sometimes these opinions are **biased**. They are conclusions that, if correct, would benefit the person in some way. In the example below, gamekeepers blamed owls for shortages of pheasants. A scientist had to look at the evidence to see if it supported the gamekeepers' conclusion.

Evidence saves the Little Owl

Just before the start of the 20th century, a few pairs of Little Owl were introduced into Britain. By the 1930s they were widespread and being accused of killing wild birds and the chicks of game birds such as pheasants. Gamekeepers killed Little Owl when they got the chance and wanted them to be wiped out entirely.

29 What did gamekeepers say about the Little Owl?

30 The bird was on trial. What sort of evidence was needed to prove whether it was guilty or innocent? Hint: Look at the pictures.

Little Owl are predators. In 1935, no one knew what they actually preyed upon.

In 1935, the British Trust for Ornithology set up an enquiry to look for evidence of what the Little Owl actually ate. The trust asked Alice Hibbert-Ware, a naturalist who had actually made observations of Little Owl and dissected their pellets, to find the answer. First, she did experiments on captive owls to find out if what was in the pellets matched what the owls had eaten. She found that it did. Then she analysed samples sent to her from dozens of places. These included 2460 pellets, 76 nest holes and 28 gizzards. A gizzard is the part of a bird's stomach where food is ground up.

What Alice found in the pellets was a mixture of fur and bones of rodents, and the hard parts of insects and worms. She found the remains of birds in the nest hole of only one Little Owl. She also received reports from gamekeepers about the loss of game birds to owls. Landowners reported that their gamekeepers had explained the shortage of pheasants because Little Owl had eaten many of the chicks.

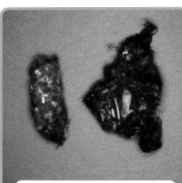

The Little Owl regurgitates pellets containing the fur and bones, and other parts that it can't digest.

31 In the passage about the Little Owl, find an example of:

  a Hearsay – what one person reports what another person said. Courts don't accept hearsay; it is not evidence;

  b A biased opinion – where a particular idea is useful to someone;

  c Valid evidence.

32 The evidence from the pellets and the reports from the gamekeepers didn't match. What was it about Alice's work that made the British Trust for Ornithology accept her conclusions that the Little Owl was not a pest, but was a useful bird?

33 A possible conclusion about the information sent in by the gamekeepers and landowners was that it consisted of biased opinions. Why might these people want to believe that the Little Owl preyed on game birds?

Why might people be biased?

In experimental investigations, you are probably used to evaluating the number and accuracy of readings and know how to deal with readings that don't fit the pattern. You assume that the work of other people who contributed results is accurate and honest. In some other investigations, for example life-style surveys, people don't always tell the truth.

34 What do we call a result that doesn't fit the pattern? Hint: You looked at this in Year 8.

35 a Sometimes smokers deny that they smoke. Suggest reasons.

b Write down <u>three</u> other lifestyle or health issues where people sometimes hide the truth.

Sonia and David investigated the variability in weight of the people in their class. They asked everyone to weigh themselves and report back. The results of a check on a random sample of weights given to them are in the table.

Person	Weight reported (N)	Weight measured [average of 3 tries] (N)	Change (N)
a	312	304	–8
b	501	518	+17
c	355	350	– 5
d	427	427	0
e	377	370	– 7
f	479	490	+11
g	432	433	+ 1
h	360	356	– 4
i	446	447	+ 1
j	384	372	– 12

36 Suggest why Sonia and David checked a sample of the weights given to them.

37 a Which <u>four</u> people's measurements are the most inaccurate?

b Suggest <u>two</u> possible reasons for the inaccuracies.

38 David saw a pattern in the results. The heaviest people had given readings that were less than their actual weight.

a What had the lightest people done?

b Suggest why they might have done that.

So, sometimes evidence is gathered inaccurately and sometimes it is incomplete. When your evidence is incomplete, you may find that your explanation turns out to be wrong. This shows just how careful you have to be when you consider and evaluate evidence.

Perhaps some people forgot to zero the scales - or perhaps they can't read them properly.

I think the difference may be something to do with how people feel about their weight.

Both these ideas could be correct.

Glossary/Index

Words in *italics* are themselves defined in the glossary.

carbon dioxide   a gas in the air produced by living things in *respiration*, in *combustion* or *burning* and when an *acid reacts* with a *carbonate*   14-15, 24, 27-28, 34-36, 38, 41, 47, 49, 55, 82-84, 89-95, 102-104, 106

carbonates   *compounds* that *react* with *acids* to produce *carbon dioxide*; *limestone* is calcium carbonate   55, 57, 77, 80

carbon monoxide   a poisonous gas   16, 84-85, 94-95

catalytic converter   in a car exhaust system, it changes nitrogen monoxide and *carbon monoxide* pollutants to nitrogen and *carbon dioxide*   77, 84-85, 91

cell (in physics)   uses a chemical *reaction* to push an *electric current* around an *electric circuit*   92, 97, 100, 106, 110-111, 116

characteristics   the special features of a plant or animal   1, 3-8, 11-12

chemical change, reaction   a *reaction* between chemicals; it produces a new substance   67, 90, 92,99, 102

chemical energy   *energy* stored in *fuels* and food   107-108, 110-111, 116

chlorophyll   the green substance in *chloroplasts* which traps *light energy*   26, 29-30, 36, 41

chloroplast   where *photosynthesis* happens in plant cells; the parts that contain *chlorophyll*   27, 29, 36

chromosome   structure made of *genes* found in the nucleus of a cell   1, 3-4, 12

cilia   tiny hairs that move back and forth; found on the surface of some cells   17

climate change   changes in climate patterns such as those caused by *global warming*   35, 77, 90

clone   a group of genetically identical living things   1, 10-12

combustion   when substances *react* with oxygen and release *energy*; another word for *burning*   92-94, 96, 99, 104-106, 149

compete, competition   when several plants or animals are trying to get the same things   37, 49

complete combustion   when a substance *burns* completely, becoming totally oxidised   43, 93, 106

components   *devices* used in *electric circuits*   107, 109-110,116

compound   a substance made from the atoms of two or more different *elements* joined together   67, 69, 92-93, 96

compress   to squeeze into a small space   145, 148-149

compressible   able to be squeezed into a small space   145, 150, 158

conclusion   what you have found out   159, 166, 167

conduction   in heat conduction, *energy* passes along a solid as its particles heat up and vibrate faster. A conductor of heat energy will let heat energy pass through it

in electrical conduction, an *electric current* flows though a substance   50-52

conservation   preserving or taking care of living things and their habitats   27, 35, 44

conservation of mass   a scientific law stating that no loss of *mass* happens in a chemical *reaction*   92, 103-106

constellation   a group of stars that forms a pattern   117, 120-121

consumer   an animal that cannot make its own food, but eats plants and other animals   37

contract   become smaller; solids, liquids and gases do this when they cool

muscles become shorter and fatter when they contract   15, 23, 154

control   part of an investigation that is needed to make a test fair; it is needed so that we can be sure of the cause of a change or a difference   30

Copernicus, Nicolaus   1473-1543   122

coronary heart disease   disorder of the coronary arteries that take blood to the heart muscles   13, 24, 26

corrosion   what happens to metals when they *react* with chemicals such as *acids* or with water and oxygen   62, 77, 81, 91

crop   amount of food or other useful *material* produced by the animals or plants that we grow   42, 44-46, 48

cuttings   parts of plants cut from an older plant and grown into new plants that are clones of the old plant   10

data   information   85-86, 88

Davy, Humphrey   1778-1829   72

deceleration   the amount by which *speed* decreases in one second; slowing down   129, 136, 144

deficiency disease   a disorder caused by a lack of a particular *nutrient* in the diet; scurvy is an example   19

Democritus   about 460-370BC   121

density   the *mass* per *unit* volume of a substance   50-51

device   something that changes *energy* from one form into another   107, 109, 116

diaphragm   a sheet of muscle that separates your chest cavity from your abdomen   15

dilute   a dilute solution contains very little dissolved solute   99

disease   when some part of a plant or animal is not working properly   48

displacement reaction   when a more *reactive element* pushes a less reactive element out of one of its *compounds*   62, 66, 68, 76, 98, 106

drag   the *friction* force acting on an object moving through air or water   129, 140-144

driving force   the force that makes something move   138-139

drug   a substance that can change the way that your body works or to treat a *disease*   13, 20-21, 23, 24, 26, 100-102

efficiency   the fraction, or percentage, of the *energy* supplied that is transformed into the desired form of energy   113

effort   the size of a force applied   145, 156-158

elastic potential energy   *energy* stored in things that are stretched or squashed   108

electrical appliance   a *device* that requires an input of *electrical energy*   109, 111-114

electrical energy   the *energy* in wires when *electric current* flows   107-112, 115

electric circuit   *components* connected together to allow an *electric current* to flow   109-110, 114, 116

electric current   flows around a complete *electric circuit*   109-110, 112, 114 - 116

electricity substation   where the *voltage* is lowered before electricity is transmitted to homes   111, 114, 116

electrochemical series   a list of metals in order of the *voltages* produced when they are used in *cells*   92, 98, 106

electrolysis   the process of splitting up a melted or dissolved *compound* by passing an *electric current* through it   62, 72, 76

element   a substance that can't be split into anything simpler by chemical *reactions*   52-53, 56, 61, 63, 67, 69, 92, 96-97, 101

emissions   pollutant gases given out from car exhausts, *power stations* etc.   84, 87, 91 emphysema   a disorder in which a person doesn't take in enough oxygen as a result of damage to the air sacs in the lungs   13, 17, 26

energy   energy is needed to make things happen   14, 19, 26, 30-32, 34, 36-40, 47, 92, 94, 102, 106-107, 116-117

energy transfer   *energy* moving from one place to another   107, 113, 116

energy transformation   when *energy* changes from one type to another   107-109, 113-114, 116

environment   the surroundings or conditions in which plants and animals live   2, 5, 12, 35, 47, 48-49, 62

environmental conditions   conditions such as light and temperature in the *environment*   5, 7, 47

environmental variations   differences within a *species* caused by the *environment*   1, 2, 12

erosion   wearing away of rocks involving the movement of the rock fragments away from where they formed   77, 91

evaluation   considering whether there is enough *evidence* to support a *conclusion* and whether an investigation can be improved   159, 166

evaporate, evaporation   when a liquid changes into a gas   53, 55-56, 58

evidence   *observations* and measurements on which theories are based   159-168

fair test   a test in which one variable is varied and other variables are controlled or kept the same   5, 75

fertilisation   when a male sex cell nucleus joins with a female sex cell nucleus to start a new plant or animal   1, 4, 6, 9, 12

fertilisers   you add these to soil to provide the minerals that plants need to grow   37, 41-42, 47-49, 100

filter, filtration   separating a liquid from undissolved solids by passing it through tiny holes, usually in paper   53, 55-56

fire triangle   a diagram showing the three things, *fuel*, heat and oxygen, needed to make a fire   96

fit   able to do a lot of exercise without tiring   13-14, 24-26

formula   uses symbols to show how many atoms of *elements* are joined together to form a molecule of an element or a *compound*   96

fossil fuels   *fuels* formed in the Earth's crust from the remains of living things; for example coal   83, 107-108, 114-115

friction   a force when two surfaces rub past each other; it acts in the opposite direction to the direction in which something is moving   96, 134, 137-141, 144,

fuel   a substance that *burns* to release *energy*   83, 92-93, 95-96, 100, 104, 115-117, 119, 140

fungicide   a substance that kills fungi   37, 57

Galileo Galilei   1564-1642   122

generator   produces electricity when it is supplied with *kinetic energy*   107, 114-116

genes   parts of *chromosomes* that control the *inherited characteristics* of plants and animals   1, 3, 6, 10, 12

geostationary orbit   an *orbit* in which a *satellite* stays above the same point on the Earth's surface, all the time   117, 125-126, 128

global warming   increase in the average temperature on Earth   35, 77, 88, 90-91

gravitational potential energy   *energy* stored in objects high up   108

gravity, gravitational force, pull   the attraction of bodies towards each other   117-119, 123-124, 128, 134, 136, 142

greenhouse effect   the warming effect on the Earth of *greenhouse gases* in the *atmosphere*;

without it, the Earth would be much colder   77, 89, 91

greenhouse gases   gases such as *methane* and *carbon dioxide* that stop some of the heat escaping from the *atmosphere*   35

haematite   an *ore* of iron; an *oxide*   62, 70, 76

hazard warning sign   tell you if a chemical is dangerous e.g. flammable or *corrosive*   58

Herschel, Caroline   1750-1845   122

Herschel, William   1738-1822   122

Hippocrates   born between 450 and 460 BC   101

Hopkins, Sir Frederick Gowland   1861-1947   18

humus   the decaying organic *material* in soil   77

hydraulic systems   a system that uses moving liquid to work, car brakes are an example   145, 151, 158

hydrocarbon   a *compound* that contains the *elements carbon* and hydrogen only   92-93, 95, 106

incomplete combustion   when a substance doesn't *burn* completely because of lack of oxygen   92-93, 95, 106

incompressible   cannot be squeezed into a smaller space   145, 150, 158

indicator organisms   plants and animals whose presence or absence shows how polluted a habitat is   77, 86

inhale   breathe in   15

inherit, inheritance   passing on of *genes* from parents   1-12

inherited characteristics   features that are inherited, or passed on from parents   1-2, 5, 12

insulate, insulation, insulator   (of heat energy) *material* that does not conduct heat; it prevents heat loss

(of *electrical energy*) *material* that does not allow an electric current to flow   51, 125

iodine solution   a test for *starch*; presence indicated by a blue-black colour   29-30

irrigation   supplying water to a *crop*   48-49

joint   where two bones meet   23-24, 154

joule, J   *energy* or work is measured in *units* called joules   111-112

Kepler, Johannes   1571-1630   122

kilowatts   1000 watts   112

kinetic energy   *energy* in a moving object   107-110, 113-114

Lavoisier, Antoine   1743-1794   105

Leonardo da Vinci   1452-1519   143

lever   used to amplify a force; an example is an oar   145, 154-158

lichens   plants made of a fungus and green algae; indicator plants for air pollution   86

ligament   tissue that holds bones together at *joints*

light energy   *energy* that luminous objects give out   108-109,

limestone   a sedimentary rock made from calcium *carbonate*   77, 80

limewater   a solution used to test for *carbon dioxide*; carbon dioxide turns the clear solution cloudy   55

load   the resistance that a force overcomes   145, 156-158

low polar orbit   an *orbit* of a *satellite* close to the Earth; the satellite scans the Earth's surface several times a day   117, 126, 128

malnutrition   eating a diet with too much or too little of particular *nutrients*   13, 19, 26

mass   the amount of stuff something is made of   103-106, 117, 119, 128

preliminary tests   tests, *trial* runs and information searches carried out to find out the best approach to an investigation   159-160

pressure   how much pushing force there is on an area   145-149, 150-158

Priestley, Joseph   1733-1804   30, 105

producer   a name given to green plants because they produce food   37

product   a new substance made in a chemical *reaction*   59, 67, 93, 103

progressive depletion   gradual decrease in the number and variety; often of living things   82

proteins   *nutrients* needed for growth and repair; made up of amino acids   18-19, 26, 31, 35-36, 38-41, 100

Ptolemy   about AD 90-168   121

pure   contains one *material* only   67-68, 79

pylon   structures that support the overhead electrical cables that are part of the *National Grid*   107, 111, 114

radiation (of heat)   a method of heat transfer, where the heat *energy* is given out as infra-red waves   89

random sample   a small part, selected at random, investigated to get an idea of the whole   168

react, reaction   what happens when chemicals join or separate   53-56, 58-59, 61-67, 69, 72, 76, 84, 96-97, 103, 106

reactant   a substance that you start off with in a chemical *reaction*   56, 102

reactive   *reacts* easily   63-4, 69, 72, 75-76

reactivity   how likely a substance is to *react*   62, 69, 74, 76, 97

reactivity series   a list of *elements* in order of how *reactive* they are   62, 64-68, 74-76

relax   in the case of a muscle, becoming longer and thinner; the opposite of *contract*   15, 23

relevant evidence   *evidence* that helps to answer a particular question   162

reliable evidence   *evidence* based on sufficient and accurate *data*   77, 85, 162

renewables   *energy* sources that are constantly being replaced so will not run out   83

respiration   the breakdown of food to release *energy* in living cells   13-15, 26, 31-32, 34, 36, 38-39, 41, 89

root hairs   tiny hairs on some root cells through which roots absorb water and minerals   27, 32, 36

rust, rusting   the *corrosion* of iron in the presence of water and oxygen to form iron *oxide*, or rust   66, 81

salt   a *compound* produced when an *acid reacts* with a metal or an *alkali*   53-58, 61-62, 65, 67-68, 75-76

satellite   a body *orbiting* a *planet*   117, 123-128

selective breeding   breeding only from the plants or animals which have the *characteristics* that we want; also called artificial selection   1, 6-8, 12, 48

series circuit   *components* connected in just one loop   110

sexual reproduction   reproduction in which the *nuclei* of two sex cells join to start a new life   10-11

sodium hydroxide   a *compound* that dissolves in water to make an *alkali*   58

solar panel   these produce electricity when *energy* is transferred to them by light   48, 125

sound energy   *energy* given out by anything that makes a noise   109, 113

species   we say that plants or animals which can interbreed belong to the same species   1, 5, 6

speed   distance travelled in a certain time   128-144

Acknowledgements

We are grateful to the following for permission to use photographs:

The Advertising Archives 23; **Alamy** 50tr (Pictor/ImageState), 73m (Ethel Davies), 73bm (Leslie Garland); **Art Directors and Trip Photo Library** 96l (Helene Rogers), 126 (NASA), 156b (Roger Chester); **Paul Beard Photo Agency** 137; **Anthony Blake Photo Library** 38 (Sian Irvine); **Catalyst Science Discovery Centre** 87b; **Cephas Picture Library** 5t (Ted Stefanski); **Corbis** 1b (Rob and Sas), 2m (Henry Diltz), 6t (Tom Nebbia), 6b (Yann Arthus-Bertrand), 7br (Picimpact), 7bl (Jim Craigmyle), 11 (Najah Feanny), 13tl (Lawrence Manning), 13tm (Roy Morsch), 13tr (David Pollack), 13bm (Tom and Dee Ann McCarthy), 13br (Tim Kiusalaas), 43b (Danny Lehman), 48tr (Nik Wheeler), 48mr (Julia Waterlow), 57tl (Michael Freeman), 57tr, 57br (Ted Speigel), 66t (Galen Rowell), 70 (Robert Holmes), 73t (Michael S. Yamashita), 73mt (Charles D.Winters), 78b (Pat O'Hara), 80mt (David Muench), 84 (Document General Motors/Reuters), 86br (Steve Austin), 87l (Michael Maslan Historical Photographs), 87tr (Michael Nicholson), 94, 96r, 98l (Richard T Nowitz), 98r (Adam Woolfit), 105 (Archivo Iconografico S.A.), 109mr, 111 (Charles Mauzy), 130t, 130mb, 130bl (Tom Brakefield), 131 (Philippe Giraud), 156m (Charles O'Rear); **Ecoscene** 82tr (Nick Hawkes), 85 (Vicki Coombs), 86m (l-r) (Chinch Gryniewicz), (Judyth Platt), (Sally Morgan), 95tr (Vicki Coombs); **Empics Sports Photo Agency** 139 (Neil Simpson); **Fisher Scientific** 60; **Getty Images** 121 (Jeremy Walker); **Philip Harris Scientific Instruments** 86tr,109l(t-b); **Holt Studios** 39 (Duncan Smith), 42 (Nigel Cattlin), 43tl (Nigel Cattlin), 43tr (Nigel Cattlin), 44t (Nigel Cattlin), 48bl (Nigel Cattlin), 57tml (Inga Spence); **Andrew Lambert** 63t, 63b, 71(all); **Nigel Luckhurst** 81tr; **Vanessa Miles** 41l, 41r, 57tmr, 57bm, 66m, 77r, 77m, 80mb, 81tl, 81br, 104,109tr, 109br, 112t, 112b, 130br, 152; **Nature Picture Library** 77l (Premaphotos); **Natural History Photo Library** 166t (Manfred Danegger), 166b (Roger Tidman); **Photofusion** 80b (Peter Olive); **Professional Sport UK Ltd** 82tm (John Babb); **Science Photo Library** 1t (Gary Parker), 2t (Alex Bartel), 2b (Mike Bluestone), 7t (John Heseltine), 7mr (Rosenfeld Images Ltd), 13bl (Erika Craddock), 17l (Matt Meadows), 17r (Matt Meadows), 19l (St. Mary's Hospital Medical School), 19r (Biophoto Associates), 21tr (Eamonn McNulty), 21br (CC Studio), 24 (Damien Lovegrove), 25t (Dave Reede), 25m (Gaillard Jerrican), 25b (Conor Coffrey), 44b (David M. Campione), 46 (B.W.Hoffman), 50r (Simon Lewis), 50br (Charles D Winters), 50bm (George Bernard), 50bl (Erich Schremp), 50ml (Sheila Terry), 50tl (Lawrence Lawry), 57bl (Dr Jeremy Burges), 69 (Jerry Mason), 72 (Sheila Terry), 73mt (Charles D. Winters), 73b (Alan Sirulnikoff), 78t (Martyn F. Chillmaid), 80t (Adam Hart-Davis), 82mb (Wesley Bocxe), 82bl (BSIP Chassenet), 82br (James King-Holmes), 93 (Richard Folwell), 95m (BSIP Chassenet), 95bl (Adam Hart-Davis), 95bm (Magrath Photography), 101l (Alfred Pasieka), 101r (Philippe Plailly), 114t (Sheila Terry), 114b (Martin Bond), 127t (Space Telescope Science Institute), 156t (Maximilian Stock Ltd); **Still Pictures** 95br (David Woodfall); **Wellcome Photolibrary** 21l; **Elizabeth Whiting Associates** 107 (Tim Street-Porter).

Picture research: Vanessa Miles

The publisher has made every effort to trace copyright holders, but if they have inadvertently overlooked any they will be pleased to make the necessary arrangements at the earliest opportunity.